Longman

CW00850581

Cars
A consumer's guide

Jacqui King

Longman

Longman Group UK Limited,
Longman House, Burnt Mill, Harlow,
Essex CM20 2JE, England
and Associated Companies throughout the world.

© Longman Group UK Limited 1987
All rights reserved; no part of this publication
may be reproduced, stored in a retrieval system,
or transmitted in any form or by any means, electronic,
mechanical, photocopying, recording, or otherwise,
without the prior written permission of the Publishers.

First published 1987

British Library Cataloguing in Publication Data

King, Jacqui
    Cars.——(Longman self-help guides)
    1. Automobiles
    I. Title
    629.2′222   TL151

    ISBN 0-582-91615-1

Set in Linotron Plantin 10/12 point.
Printed in Great Britain
by Butler and Tanner Ltd, Frome, Somerset

ABOUT THE AUTHOR

Since setting up a Consumer Advice Centre in East London, Jacqui King has for the last five years been manager of an Advice Centre in South London. In addition to this, she is Research and Information Officer for the Institute of Consumer Advisers, has written numerous leaflets on consumer rights, lectured regularly on consumer law to advice workers, colleges, consumer organisations and the retail sector, and made a number of appearances on radio and television.

Dedication

Ticka, if this can entice you from two to four wheels, it will not have been in vain.

Contents

Introduction

My experience as a consumer adviser has led me to the conclusion that, whilst any consumer complaint is problematic, the buying, selling and repairing of cars seems to cause more headaches than most.

Some would argue that part of the problem relates to the fact that there is a high percentage of 'cowboys' in the motor trade. Whilst there is possibly some truth in this contention, consumers themselves are by no means blameless. The majority of problems arise because consumers frequently take less care in the purchase of a car than they would in the purchase of a pair of shoes. Considering the expense involved, never mind the possible safety risk, it is an extraordinary fact of life that consumers can be so careless over such a major purchase.

In addition, the very fact that there are so many things which can go wrong with a car makes the whole business complicated and confusing. Traders often try to 'blind you with science' – using terminology which most consumers simply don't understand. This is even more true when it comes to servicing and repairs and many consumers are loath to admit that they really don't understand what goes on under the bonnet. Thus, they leave themselves wide open to be 'ripped off'.

Many problems can be avoided if consumers have a basic understanding not only of the fundamental workings of a car and the terminology, but also of the law relating to motorists and of rights and obligations regarding consumer contracts. Often, consumers are not specific when they enter into contracts – they do not make their requirements clear; they do not fix time limits; and they are not clear about the cost involved.

On top of this, consumers may then find themselves completely lost in the maze of insurance when they have to make a claim.

Hopefully, most of these problems have been simplified in this book. It is not possible to cover every situation but experience has given me a fairly good insight into the most common problems and the best ways of resolving them, either through legal action or by negotiation.

Some legislation, particularly that relating to credit, is very complicated. I have tried, wherever I think it helpful, to give examples in order to clarify complex points. I have also tried to make it easy for you to 'dip in', in order to deal with a single problem where necessary. I envisage the book being used more as easy reference than as light bedtime reading!

Cars: A consumer's guide developed out of a specialised training course given by the Institute of Consumer Advisers, of which I was until recently chairman.

I produced detailed course notes to complement the training course and the Institute received so many requests for copies of the course notes that they eventually published the notes in the form of a booklet. That booklet formed the basis of this book and thanks are due to the Institute of Consumer Advisers for its permission to use the booklet in this way.

A number of individuals have been very helpful in providing information and assistance in the compiling of this book. I am especially grateful to Gill Miller for her extraordinary ability to translate my dictation and scribble into a beautifully typed manuscript and I would also like to thank the following:

Harry Jones	Society of Motor Manufacturers and Traders
John Lepine	Motor Schools Association of Great Britain
Ted Dewbery	Association of British Insurers
Harry Brisco	Automobile Association

Robert Van Dissel	Institute of Advanced Motorists
Liz Purdie	DVLC Information Branch
Sirkkaliisa Levonen	Action on Alcohol Abuse
James Powell	
P. C. Terry West	Southwark Crime Prevention Officer
Dick Reeves	Scotland Yard

Acknowledgements

We are grateful to the following for permission to reproduce copyright material:

Crown copyright, reproduced with the permission of the controller of Her Majesty's Stationery Office for pages 15 (top) and 167 (bottom); The Institute of Advanced Motorists for page 233 (top); Motor Agents Association for pages 53 and 233 (lower top); The Motor Schools Association of Great Britain, Salford, Manchester, Tel. 061-736 1515 for page 233 (upper middle); Scottish Motor Trade Association for page 233 (lower middle); The Society of Motor Manufacturers and Traders Ltd for page 233 (upper bottom); The Vehicle Builders and Repairers Association for page 233 (bottom).

The motor car

Technical terminology

Many people 'switch off' when technical terminology is used –
especially if they are unable to visualise 'big ends' or 'crankshafts'
and understand their functions. So this chapter is designed to be a
very basic look at the engine. Numbers used in the following
paragraphs refer to the diagrams overleaf.

Petrol and air are taken into the cylinder (49) and compressed. The
mixture is ignited by a spark from a sparking plug (29), thus heating
the air, which then expands. Inside each cylinder is a piston (47)
which slides freely up and down. Each piston is joined to a
connecting rod (44) which in turn connects to the crankshaft (41).
Most engines have four cylinders, housed in a box, the top half of
which is called the cylinder block (52) and the bottom half the
crankcase (51). In the majority of engines the cylinder block and
crankcase are all one piece – known as the 'block'. Power, supplied
when starting by the battery (6), provides the spark through the
ignition system, via the coil (4), distributor (33) and sparking plugs
(29).

Engines will get very hot so the heat is controlled by the cooling
system. Some engines are air-cooled but most are water-cooled: the
water is cooled in the radiator (9), assistd by a fan (28), and the
temperature is controlled by a thermostat (35).

The function of the transmission is to transmit the power supplied
by the engine to the wheels. It incorporates the steering gear (14),
clutch (12) and brakes (15), gearbox (1), propeller shaft (17) and
final drive (19). There are two main types of brakes on most cars:
drum brakes (21) (22) and disc brakes (11). Either or both may be
fitted, but usually the disc brakes are on the front wheels.

2

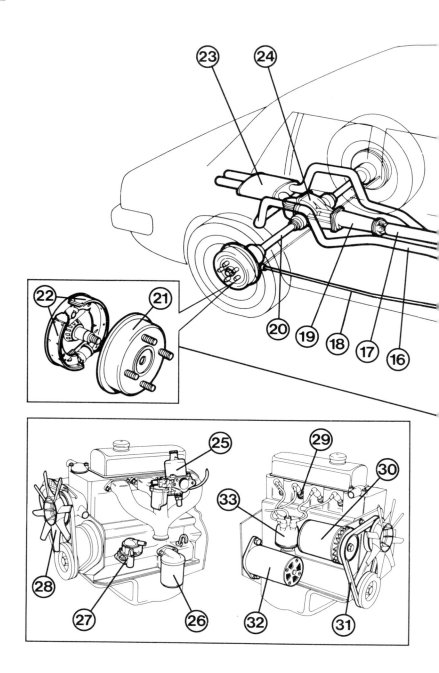

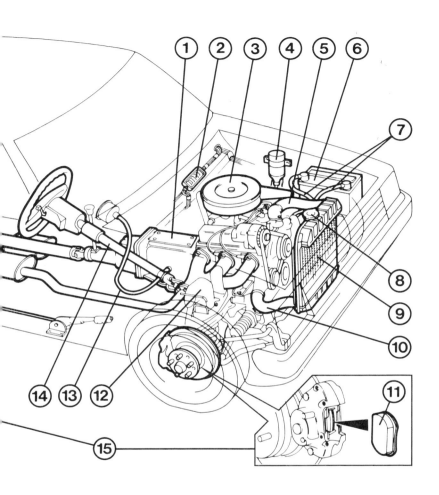

1 gearbox	12 clutch	24 differential
2 fuse box	13 speedometer cable	25 carburettor
3 air filter	14 steering column	26 oil filter
4 coil	15 brakes	27 fuel pump
5 radiator hose (top)	16 exhaust pipe	28 fan
6 battery	17 propeller shaft	29 sparking plug
7 battery leads	18 hand brake cable	30 alternator
8 filler cap (radiator)	19 final drive	31 fan belt
9 radiator	20 rear axle	32 starter motor
10 radiator hose (bottom)	21 brake drum	33 distributor
	22 brake shoe	34 water pump
11 disc brake pad	23 silencer	35 thermostat

4

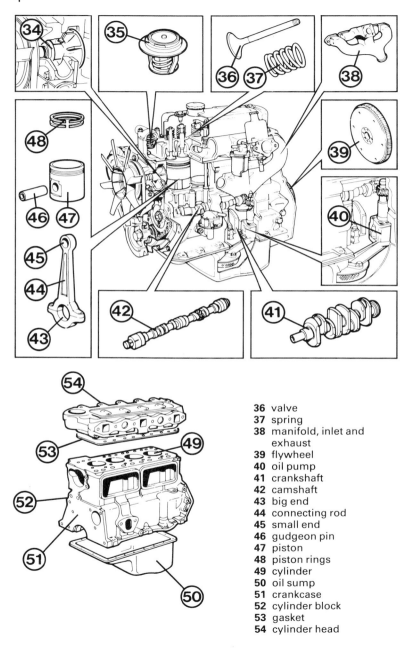

36 valve
37 spring
38 manifold, inlet and
exhaust
39 flywheel
40 oil pump
41 crankshaft
42 camshaft
43 big end
44 connecting rod
45 small end
46 gudgeon pin
47 piston
48 piston rings
49 cylinder
50 oil sump
51 crankcase
52 cylinder block
53 gasket
54 cylinder head

The foregoing paragraphs are intended to be nothing more than a way of familiarising you with technical terminology which you can 'picture'. There are many detailed books available if your appetite has been whetted and specific handbooks can be purchased for virtually all makes and models.

Turbo-charged engines

These are becoming popular as a means of giving the smaller sporty car a bit more power. The turbo-charge extracts the waste that would normally disappear down the exhaust pipe and converts it to additional energy in order to provide more power and to increase the efficiency of the engine.

Turbo-charged engines, therefore, should be more powerful in relation to the size of the engine and they should also run more efficiently, thus proving more economical.

Diesel

The sale of diesels has doubled since 1982 and more and more models are becoming available, so let us look at some of the advantages and disadvantages.

Disadvantages

In general, diesels are considered to be 'heavier' to handle. This is because diesel engines are relatively less powerful. The boost which you may need to overtake, for example, may be disappointing to say the least, and this 'slowness' could take some getting used to. Another disadvantage may be the availability of fuel. Although it is becoming more widely stocked, you may still have difficulty in finding a garage that sells it if you are in the country. At petrol stations that are not self service, do make sure that the attendant does not fill your car up with the wrong fuel. It is most important to ensure a diesel does not run out of fuel completely. Some may need special attention to be restarted. You may have to unscrew a plunger near the fuel injection pump and pump it manually. Some models need to be bled before you can pump them.

The wax contained in diesel fuel can cause problems too. In very cold weather it may separate and clog the filters. This is likely to happen if temperatures fall below 9°C.

There is no doubt that diesels are smellier and noisier than other models, although there have been major improvements in noise reduction over the last five years or so.

Finally, most diesel cars need servicing more frequently than similar petrol models and they are more expensive to buy.

Advantages

The advantages probably do not outweigh the disadvantages but they are worth considering. To begin with, diesel is usually cheaper than petrol. Also diesel engines are far more efficient than an equivalent petrol-run car in terms of fuel economy, so running costs will be lower.

When it comes to selling your diesel car, you will find that some models depreciate less than petrol models and so the resale value would be relatively better.

If you are concerned about environmental pollution, it is worth noting that diesel fuel does not contain lead.

Despite all the criticisms levelled against them, the sales of diesel cars have increased fairly dramatically over the last two years or so and they now account for roughly 4.5 per cent of the total UK market. They are more popular in Europe though, where the total market figures for 1984 were: Italy 26 per cent; France 14 per cent; Belgium 20 per cent; Germany 13 per cent. In 1984, the UK figure was only 2.6 per cent, representing 45,000 sales. By 1986 the number of sales had increased to 81,000.

Tyres

There are two main types of tyres, crossply and radial.

Construction

Between the rubber tread and the inner lining of tyres there are two to four layers (or casing plies) of cord made of rayon or nylon.

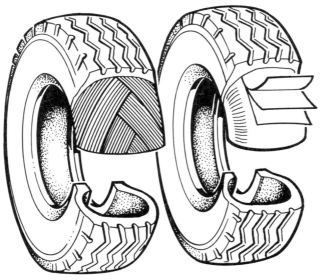

Crossply   Radial

Crossply tyres were first introduced in the early 1920s. Previously, tyres were made of woven canvas and were not suited to high speeds because they overheated and frayed.

Crossplies are so named because the casing plies below the tread go diagonally across the tyre, crossing at an angle of about 40 degrees.

Radials were first introduced in 1948 by Michelin. The casing plies on a radial tyre consist of one layer going straight around the tyre following the radius (hence the name) and several tread bracing plies between the tread and casing ply which follow the circumference of the tyre. This design prevents the walls of the tyre from remaining too rigid and thus as the walls flex so more tread remains on the road, giving better grip.

Steel-braced radials are the same basic design as standard radials but the tread bracing plies are made of steel cord.

Radials are more expensive but give better grip and their construction ensures reduced wear when cornering. They can last between 50 and 100 per cent longer than crossplies.

Remould tyres

These are cheaper than new tyres because they are, in fact, secondhand tyres on which all of the rubber has been renewed and remoulded.

Retread tyres

These are also cheaper but are a false economy if a high mileage is expected because the tread has just been re-cut into a worn tyre thus, obviously, making them thinner.

Remould quality

Tyres marked 'remould quality' are new tyres which are slightly sub-standard and can be a very good buy.

Fitting

Different types or sizes of tyres must *never* be fitted to the same axle of a vehicle.

It is alright to fit crossply tyres on the front wheels and radials on the rear but, because of the different cornering ability of the two types, it is highly dangerous the other way round. Equally, it is dangerous to fit steel-braced radials at the front and textile-braced radials at the rear.

The legal minimum tread depth is 1 mm all over the tyre.

Denovo tyres

Denovo tyres are becoming increasingly popular.

They are similar to a radial and can also be steel-braced. However, the side walls are thicker and the inside is lubricated with a substance called Polygell which also acts as a sealant.

In approximately 70 per cent of punctures, the sealant moves into the hole before all of the air escapes, thus enabling the driver to continue safely. In the case of the other 30 per cent, the hole is usually too large for the Polygell to be effective, in which case the 'Denloc Principle' comes into effect. This means that the wheel will remain stable instead of collapsing thereby enabling the driver to maintain control of the car. One of the biggest problems with conventional tyres is that when they go flat, they dislodge from the wheel. This is not possible with Denovos.

The major advantages then are those of safety and convenience. You can continue to drive on a Denovo for a distance of 100 miles at speeds not in excess of 50 mph before either having the tyre repaired or changed. There is a British Standard for the repair of Denovos.

Denovos cannot be fitted to standard wheels however, and they are approximately 30 per cent more expensive than conventional tyres although the life expectancy is about the same (ie about 20,000–24,000 miles, depending on how the car is driven).

Spare wheels

You are not legally obliged to carry a spare wheel. However, if one is carried it must not be defective.

Spacesavers

Some car manufacturers have recently taken to supplying a special type of spare wheel with new vehicles. They are called 'Spacesavers', for obvious reasons, and they are smaller and thinner than conventional tyres.

The basis of the idea is to provide extra room in the boot whilst still carrying a spare but these tyres are not meant to be replacements, rather a means of enabling you to continue your journey, after a puncture, far enough to have the proper tyre repaired or replaced. Logically of course, they could be a disadvantage. If you have a boot full of luggage when you have to change the wheel where are you going to store the wheel you have just taken off?

Like damaged Denovos, it is not recommended that they be used for more than 100 miles or if travelling at more than 50 mph.

Motoring organisations and some mechanics have expressed severe reservations about both the use of these tyres and about their production. There are fears that they may become more widely available as a cheap alternative or may even be deliberately supplied as such by unscrupulous garages.

There is no cheap alternative to safety. The type and condition of tyres is fundamental to road safety – so beware when buying tyres.

Documentation

Background

Drivers have needed licences and vehicles have needed to be registered since 1903, under the terms of the Motor Car Act.

At that time, a driving licence cost five shillings (25 pence) and was valid for a year. The licence was granted to anybody over the age of 17. No one was required to take lessons or to pass any kind of driving test and there were not even any rules regarding medical fitness. The main reason for the introduction of driving licences was for the purpose of identification.

The first kind of test which drivers were required to take applied only to disabled drivers and was introduced in 1930. It was not until 1935 that driving tests became compulsory for anyone who began driving after 1 April 1934.

The registration of vehicles, which was also introduced in 1903, was again simply a matter of identification. The registration mark would tell you where the vehicle had originally been registered and would be made up of one or two letters (identifying the county) and up to four figures. The licence was valid, as it is now, for a year although the cost was only £1. It was not until 1920 that annual and quarterly vehicle licensing came about although a type of taxation (the road fund) had been collected since 1910.

By 1930 the number of registrations was so great that the registration marks changed to consist of three letters and three figures, and by the middle of the 1950s, 'reverse' marks began in order to provide more registration marks. These contained three or four figures, followed by one, two or three letters which would identify the county of origin.

By 1960, so many vehicles were on the road that some authorities had run out of registration marks and so in 1963 'forward' marks were introduced which ended with a letter indicating the year that the vehicle was first registered. This system was exhausted in 1983 and so was reversed and the letter showing the year of registration is placed at the front of the registration mark.

Registration letters

The system of adding letters to a registration mark to indicate the year is known as the 'seven symbol' system. Each year has two letters because the new registration letter begins in August.

1963 A & B	1968 F & G	1973 L & M	1978 S & T	1983 Y & A
1964 B & C	1969 G & H	1974 M & N	1979 T & V	1984 A & B
1965 C & D	1970 H & J	1975 N & P	1980 V & W	1985 B & C
1966 D & E	1971 J & K	1976 P & R	1981 W & X	1986 C & D
1967 E & F	1972 K & L	1977 R & S	1982 X & Y	1987 D & E

As you can see certain letters such as 'I' and 'O' have been omitted. This was done in order to reduce the likelihood of confusion with numbers.

In August 1983, a new prefix 'Q' was introduced for vehicles which had been used in other countries prior to the first registration in the UK, such as cars which were not new but were imported. 'Q' is also used for cars where the actual date of first use or registration (in this country or abroad) cannot certainly be determined. The rest of the registration mark of such vehicles will still be appropriate to the date of registration.

The 'Q' series goes a long way to preventing consumers being deliberately misled by advertisements which refer only to the registration letter. For example, if a car is advertised as a 'Y reg' it would be reasonable for the buyer to assume it was a late 1982 or early 1983 model. But the car could easily be a couple of years older than that and imported into this country in 1982, thus receiving a 'Y' registration mark when it was first registered here.

When all of this began, the collecting of fees and the issuing of documents was carried out at local level by 181 local vehicle licensing offices, run by the local authorities. However, in the 1960s there was such an enormous increase in the number of drivers (50 per cent) and the number of vehicles (60 per cent) that the local system was becoming unable to cope with the demand. A variety of problems was recognised. For example, it was possible for a disqualified driver to obtain a driving licence simply by completing another application form at a different local office. Furthermore, the enormous amount of time spent by clerks, manually completing details on log books and transferring them from one local office to another when people moved or sold their vehicle to someone living elsewhere, was simply uneconomical.

DVLC

By 1965 the government had decided that a national, computerised centre was necessary and Swansea was chosen partly because there was sufficient space to build such an enormous complex but also, in consultation with the Department of Employment, to provide jobs in an area where there was a particularly high rate of unemployment at that time.

Although the Driver and Vehicle Licensing Centre (DVLC) deals with the majority of licensing functions, there still remain 53 local vehicle licensing offices which can allocate new registration marks, issue tax discs and collect duty, trace vehicles and enforce the law regarding untaxed vehicles.

In addition, about three thousand post offices are authorised to issue tax discs and deal with licence applications and they handle about 95 per cent of all vehicle licence applications.

The number of vehicles and drivers continues to increase (in 1950 there were 5.7 million driving licences and 4.4 million vehicles, and by 1983/4 there were 36.6 million driving licences and 28.9 million vehicles). So that the time has come for the DVLC to introduce an even more sophisticated system for dealing with their enormous workload. By 1987, their new system will be in effect so that applications and registrations can be processed within minutes of receipt and they will also be despatched much faster than they are now. However, certain applications will continue to take longer for processing. At the moment approximately 1 per cent of licence applications contain medical declarations and these must be processed separately, sometimes with reference to the applicant's doctor or to a specialist. DVLC has its own drivers' Medical Advisory Unit which employs a team of doctors to deal with these cases.

One of the most important ways in which you can ensure speedy processing of an application is to make sure you use the correct postcode. DVLC has 17 different postcodes which are designed to relate specifically to the transaction required so that mail arrives in the correct department pre-sorted.

You should also ensure that your form has been completed correctly. Approximately 3 per cent of applications have to be returned because there is an error and over 480,000 items arrive at the DVLC daily of which around 90 per cent are dealt with within 10 working days. The major work of the DVLC is to maintain a record of all people licenced to drive and to send them reminders and to maintain the central vehicle record, issuing tax discs and sending reminders. There are, however, a number of other functions which include: recording driving test passes; recording licence endorsements and disqualifications; issuing registration documents; vehicle excise duty refunds; supplying registration details to the police; enforcing payment of excise duty (evasion is estimated at about 4 per cent, which represents annual revenue loss of £90 million); and dealing with enquiries from motor manufacturers (eg for recall campaigns), the police and local authorities (eg Trading Standards Departments seeking information with a view to prosecution) and from members of the public.

Documents for the car

Before taking any vehicle on the public highway, the driver must be in possession of the following documents:

- a valid driving licence
- relevant insurance cover
- road tax

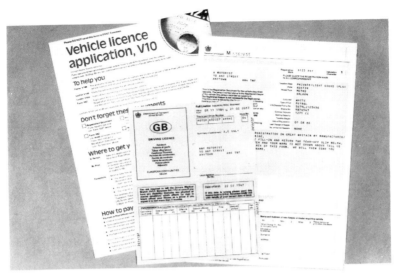

Sample DVLC documents: from left, vehicle licence application,
GB driving licence, vehicle registration document

- vehicle registration document
- MOT certificate (if the vehicle is more than three years old).

Driving licence

You must have a valid driving licence – and do not forget to sign it.

- If you have never driven before, details on how to apply for a
  provisional driving licence can be found in chapter 2.

- If you hold a current foreign driving licence or an international
  driving permit you may drive for up to a year after entering the
  country. If you intend to stay here, you must take a driving test
  as soon as possible and if you fail you will have to apply for a
  provisional licence until you have passed a British driving test.

- If you hold a driving licence issued within the EEC you may
  simply apply for a full licence, but this must be done within a
  year of arriving in this country. There is an exchange
  arrangement with certain countries who have driving standards

comparable to ours by which a new resident can simply exchange a foreign licence for a valid British one. This applies only to the following countries:

Australia	Kenya	Singapore
Barbados	Malta	Spain
British Virgin Islands	New Zealand	Sweden
Finland	Norway	Switzerland
Hong Kong	Republic of Cyprus	Zimbabwe

- The exchange must be applied for within one year of becoming resident in this country and you must surrender your current licence. The Department will require the original licence, not a copy, and you should use the standard driving licence application form (D1). The fee for an exchange licence is £3.

- If your driving licence is lost or stolen you must notify the police immediately and apply for a duplicate. This can be done using the normal driving licence application form (D1) available from any post office. The fee for a duplicate driving licence is £3. If the original licence is recovered after you have received the duplicate you must return it to the DVLC.

Vehicle insurance

It is a criminal offence to drive a car on a public highway without adequate insurance. There are basically four types of vehicle insurance:

ROAD TRAFFIC ACT
This is the minimum cover permitted by law. It covers you for injury to your passengers, passengers in other cars and pedestrians. It does not cover you for damage to your own car and, if you are responsible for the accident, other people's property.

THIRD PARTY ONLY
This provides the same cover as above plus damage to other people's vehicles and property. It does not cover the damage to your own car.

THIRD PARTY, FIRE AND THEFT
This provides the same cover as above plus cover if your car is stolen or goes up in flames.

FULLY COMPREHENSIVE

In this case you will be covered for all of the above together with the cost of any damage to your vehicle whether it is your own fault or not. You will also have cover for items stolen from inside the car – up to a maximum figure, and it may include a variety of extra benefits. For example, you may have separate windscreen cover – this means that should you need to claim for just a broken windscreen you will not lose your no claims bonus. You can also obtain 'no claims bonus protection cover' which means that you can insure against losing your full no claims bonus in the event of an accident which is not your fault. There is a variety of other types of cover available under such policies. For example, you can insure against mechanical breakdown, the cost of towing, hiring another vehicle and even for legal expenses, should you need to pursue a claim against someone responsible for an accident.

HIRE AND REWARD

This is additional cover which must be taken out if you use your vehicle to carry passengers for money, for example, mini-cab driving. You would not need this additional cover just for car-sharing (using your car to transport other people regularly, say to work, and sharing the expenses).

EXCESS

Excesses, usually of £50, £75 or £100, will be imposed by the insurance company on inexperienced drivers or those who have had a number of accidents or convictions. This means that the insured agrees to pay that much of each claim. For example, if you have an excess of £100 and you have an accident which incurs £150 worth of repairs it may not be worth your while claiming on the insurance, since you would have to pay the first £100 yourself.

Apart from excesses which are imposed by the insurance companies, you could choose to have an excess in order to reduce the cost of the insurance. The effect, of course, is the same, in the event of a claim you pay the first £x amount, the insurance company pays the balance.

In deciding whether to insure someone, the insurance company is interested only in the risk; in other words if you are inexperienced or have a bad driving record, you are a high risk and that is obviously going to put up the cost of your insurance. In order to assess the risk the insurance company needs all the relevant facts concerning the driver of the vehicle.

In deciding what kind of insurance to have, the following points must be taken into account:

- age and value of the car

- ask yourself the question: 'if my car was parked and it was demolished by someone who didn't leave their details, could I afford to write off that loss and forget about it?' If the answer is no, then fully comprehensive insurance is a must.

- cost

The price you pay for insurance depends on a number of things. Vehicles are split into groups. Usually 1 to 7, the lowest being for cars with a small engine capacity, such as Minis and Fiestas, and the highest being for sports cars, Rolls Royces, etc. Foreign cars tend to be more expensive to insure because of the cost of repairs.

The other thing taken into account is the circumstances of the driver of the vehicle. Insurance can be limited to a named driver only, that is the person named as the insured, and means that only he or she can drive the car. Named people can also be added to the policy, and their circumstances will be taken into account when deciding how much the insurance will cost. The policy could also be extended to cover any driver, but this of course would make it more expensive.

Car insurance is usually dealt with by an insurance broker and you should ensure that the broker you choose is an expert and not likely to rip you off or go bust, leaving you without cover.

Anyone can set themselves up as a broker without any qualifications or previous experience *but*, because of a law called the Insurance Brokers Registration Act, you cannot call yourself a 'broker' unless you are registered with the Insurance Brokers Registration Council. Registration will be granted only to people who are fit to trade and have indemnity which protects the client from loss if anything goes wrong.

Avoid people who call themselves 'agents' or 'consultants' and choose the one who uses the word 'broker' in the business name. Then, just to be on the safe side, telephone the IBRC and ask whether they *are* registered brokers. If they call themselves brokers and are not registered, they are committing a criminal offence and can be prosecuted. Take your business elsewhere and report them either to the IBRC or your local Trading Standards Department.

PROPOSAL FORM

Having selected your broker the first step is to complete a proposal form, which is a questionnaire designed to give the insurance company all the necessary information about the driver of the car. It is absolutely vital that when this proposal form is completed, all of the questions are answered truthfully and accurately.

Sometimes, the insurance broker will complete the form for you, in order to save time, and ask you to sign it. Do not sign it unless you have read it and ensured that all of the information which you gave was truthful and is on the form. Regardless of whether the form is completed by you or your insurance broker, it remains your responsibility once you have signed it and if any information is incorrect, it is no use blaming the insurance broker.

The proposal form will then be sent to the insurance company for them to decide whether to insure you and how much it will cost. They will keep this form on their files as a permanent record and although the information will not be checked for accuracy when it is received, if you make a claim, the insurance company will check every single detail on the proposal form before deciding whether or not to pay out. You must remember that a number of years may pass before a claim is made and therefore if your circumstances change at any time the insurance company must be informed. For instance if, after being insured for five years, you are convicted of speeding this may not necessarily affect the cost of your insurance but it certainly affects the risk. Therefore the insurance company must be told about it otherwise a future claim may not be paid. This is what insurance companies call 'non disclosure of a material fact' (see page 148). ALWAYS keep a copy of your proposal form and remember to check it from time to time and to advise the insurance company, in writing, of any changes.

COVER NOTE

Once the proposal form has been completed the insurance broker will be able to give you a rough figure of the cost of the insurance. You will pay that amount and be given a cover note. This document simply shows that you are covered for the minimum legal requirement – Road Traffic Act cover only. If, having received your proposal form, the insurance company decides the risk may be greater, they will advise the broker who will contact you and may ask for more money. Many people complain that having shopped around for the best price and paid it, the insurance company then asks for more money. This is not necessarily the fault of the broker, who is simply acting as an agent for you. Until the insurance company has seen the proposal form and decided whether or not to insure you, no contract between you and the insurance company exists. If you are asked for more money you have the right to refuse and take your business elsewhere. Remember that the moment you do that, you are not covered to drive the vehicle. You would be entitled to have your money refunded, less any time which had elapsed whilst you were on minimum cover under the cover note.

CERTIFICATE OF INSURANCE

This is not the same as a cover note. It shows that the policy has been issued and gives details of the type of cover which you have. Shortly after you receive your certificate of insurance you will receive your policy document. A new certificate of insurance will be issued each year when you renew your cover. You will not receive a new policy each year. The certificate of insurance is a very important document. It is, for example, the document that the police require should you ever be asked to produce your documents at a police station. They are not interested in cover notes as these do not prove that a policy has been issued and that you are in fact insured.

RENEWAL

Your vehicle insurance is renewable annually and if you stay with the same insurance company you will not be asked to complete a new proposal form – this is why it is so important to remember that it is your responsibility to advise the insurance company of any change in the risk. If there has been any change in your circumstances, no matter how minor and apparently irrelevant, you must advise the insurance company. You may have changed your job or found it necessary to wear spectacles, you may have been convicted of a relatively minor offence. All these things affect the risk and the insurance company must be advised in writing. These may seem like unimportant technical matters but insurance companies have refused to meet claims for just such wrong information. Each year when you renew your insurance you effectively enter into a new contract with the insurance company and therefore must treat it as if you are starting afresh.

NO CLAIMS BONUSES

After you have been insured for a year, if there have been no claims your insurance company may award a no claims bonus, usually 20 per cent for the first year. This means that when you renew, your insurance will be 20 per cent cheaper. It may not actually make a great deal of difference in cost as insurance prices also increase generally. However, if you continue to drive without any claims, your no claims bonus will continue to increase, usually to a maximum of 65 per cent.

If you have a claim during that period you will lose your no claims bonus but do check the small print on your policy as many insurance companies have agreed to withdraw the no claims bonus on a sliding scale. For example, if the claim is for damage to your vehicle after an accident which was not your fault, the insurance company may not remove the whole of your no claims bonus. Do remember though that they are entitled to withdraw the whole bonus in the event of any claim, regardless of blame.

Road tax (Road fund licence) (Vehicle excise duty)

All vehicles, whilst on the road, must be taxed and must display a tax disc. It is a criminal offence for a vehicle to be on the road without tax or if the disc is not displayed.

The vehicle licence application form (V10) is obtainable at post offices, and the address of the local vehicle licensing office is shown at the back of the form. The rates of vehicle excise duty are also available from post offices. The charges are different for motor cycles, three wheeled vehicles, goods vehicles, etc.

The disc will show the date that the road fund licence expires, the registration number and type of vehicle, whether it was taxed for six or twelve months, and the fee paid.

REFUND

The duty, or part of it, may be refunded if the vehicle is sold or scrapped. On the back of the tax disc are details of how to obtain a refund. If the vehicle has a registration document (V5) post the licence to the Driver and Vehicle Licensing Centre, Swansea, SA99 1AL, or hand it in at any local licensing office.

Once a vehicle has been registered in your name on the log book, you will automatically be sent a renewal reminder about two weeks before the tax runs out (V11). This reminder can be taken, with your insurance certificate, and MOT certificate if appropriate, to the nearest post office authorised to issue tax discs or you can send it to your nearest head post office, the address of which will be shown on the form V11. It is not necessary for you to take the registration document (log book) with you. Applications should *not* be made to a local vehicle licensing office or to DVLC.

Many people assume that if they do not have a registration document they are unable to tax a vehicle. This is not true, you can tax your car without the log book but this must be done only at a local vehicle licensing office.

Vehicle registration document (log book)

All vehicles must have a registration document (log book – form V5). The person named on the registration document is the 'registered keeper' of the vehicle. The registered keeper is not necessarily the legal owner.

The registration document will show the registration number of the vehicle, the class, make and model, the colour, the type of fuel, the chassis and engine number, the cylinder capacity, the date of the original registration of the vehicle, the date of the last change of the registered keeper of the vehicle, and the number of former keepers.

It is generally agreed that the old type of log book was preferable because of the details on it regarding previous keepers. Although the new registration document indicates the number of former keepers, it does not give details as to the use of the vehicle. For instance, if the previous owner had been a company it would be reasonable to assume that the car had been used by a company representative and therefore may not have been particularly well cared for.

SALE OR TRANSFER

At the bottom of the vehicle registration document is a section headed 'Notification of Sale or Transfer', and if the vehicle is sold or transferred to someone else this section must be completed by the present keeper, signed by the person to whom the vehicle is being transferred, torn off and sent to the DVLC. The top half of the vehicle registration document is then handed to the new keeper.

It is important to safeguard your interests by completing this section and returning it because it indicates that all responsibility for the vehicle has been taken over by someone else. The previous owner cannot then be held responsible for road tax, accidents, etc. If, for some reason, it is not possible to get the new keeper's signature, the form can be sent without it so long as you ensure that the date of transfer is completed.

MOT certificate

The compulsory testing of vehicles was first introduced in 1960 and was confined to vehicles over ten years old. Later it was reduced to five years and, in 1969, three years. It is illegal to drive a car which is three or more years old if it does not have a valid test certificate, except to drive it to a testing station for the test to be done.

A test can only be carried out by garages which have authorised examiners. Some local authorities also have testing stations and there is also a Department of Transport testing facility at Hendon which is available to the public. The testing stations may only use equipment which is approved by the Department and only persons specifically authorised to do so may carry out tests and issue test certificates.

All authorised examiners must display the following:

- the names of all nominated testers
- a notice detailing the times that the station can conduct tests
- the certificate of authorisation
- the address and telephone number of the district office to which appeals against the refusal to issue a test certificate may be sent
- a notice detailing the current test fees applicable
- the prescribed testing station sign.

An authorised examiner is held personally responsible for the action of those employees who are nominated testers and the examiner must ensure that they are properly supervised. Authorised examiners are responsible for loss, damage or injury during the time the vehicle is in their custody for testing and whilst the test is being carried out.

If you purchase a used car which has a recent test certificate and the car is subsequently found to have a number of defects, you should contact the appropriate district office nearest to where the test was carried out and they may decide to examine the car. This would only be done at their discretion since they are not legally obliged to do so. They would need to see the car within 14 days of the test being carried out for normal defects and within 12 weeks for complaints about corrosion. Any later than that would be of no use since they would have to be able to prove beyond reasonable doubt that the defects were evident at the time of the test.

If it is found that the test certificate should not have been issued, the station's authorisation could be withdrawn, but it would have to be a very serious complaint. The normal procedure is for the station to be sent a warning letter. If they have received one other warning letter in the previous five years, their authorisation may be withdrawn. In cases of carelessness the actual tester may be removed from testing. The testing station does have the right to appeal against a withdrawal of authorisation.

FORGED MOT CERTIFICATE
An individual can be arrested for being in possession of a forged MOT certificate.

The Department of Transport sells books of blank test certificates to authorised examiners. These books are worth a lot of money on the black market. The penalty for a forged test certificate is a fine but anyone found in possession of a stolen test certificate may be liable to imprisonment.

Some unscrupulous car dealers obtain cars which have failed an MOT test just before they get to the scrap heap, tidy them up, use forged or stolen test certificates and then sell the cars. The following is a list of points to look for on an MOT certificate:

- at the top of the certificate it should say 'Department of Transport' not 'Ministry of Transport' (these are the old type of certificate)

- the signature of the tester should be clear not smudged or altered

- the stamp with the garage's name and address should look professional

- at the bottom of the certificate are numbers, eg 12/85. These numbers indicate the date on which the certificate was printed. In this case, December 1985. A certificate should not be more than two years old.

- there should be no alterations to the date. It is illegal.

Any further information regarding MOT certificates can be obtained from the Vehicle Inspection Division of the Department of Transport (address on page 233).

It is important to remember that the test does not require dismantling of parts of the vehicle and, as it says on the test certificate, it 'only relates to the testable items at the time they were tested and cannot therefore normally be regarded as evidence of their condition at any other time. Nor should it be accepted as evidence of a vehicle's general condition.'

In other words, if someone buys a used car, the provision of a valid test certificate is not sufficient indication of the condition of the car at the time of purchase. It is perfectly possible for a car with a seriously defective engine to be granted a test certificate. The items checked during an MOT test are as follows:

- lights
- steering and suspension
- braking system
- tyres and wheels
- seat belts
- general items, eg windscreen wipers and washers, horn, exhaust system, structure.

Anyone driving a dangerously defective vehicle is liable to prosecution and it must also be remembered that it may invalidate your insurance.

The law

All motorists must have current documentation as outlined in this chapter. It is not, however, necessary to carry all the documents with you at all times. In fact it is not advisable to leave your documents in the car in case it is stolen.

If you are stopped by the police and asked for your documents you will be allowed up to seven days within which to produce them at a police station of your choice. Failure to produce them is an offence.

It is also an offence to alter documents. For example, to change the date on a document which has expired. Equally, documents must not be lent to anyone else or used by anyone else. For example, if you lend your driving licence to someone who, if stopped, gives a false name and address (yours) to the police, you will both be guilty of an offence.

Learning to drive

Driving lessons are not cheap these days but there is no substitute for expert tuition, and choosing a good instructor could save you money in the long run. Learning to drive with a friend or relative is not wise because all of us develop some bad driving techniques over the years and whilst they may not necessarily make us bad drivers, they are the sort of things that would fail us if we had to take a driving test again!

Experience counts for a lot but you can only get the experience after having been taught well.

Apart from being able to handle a vehicle, you must also be familiar with the highway code and you will be questioned on it during your driving test. It would also be wise to invest in a copy of *Driving* published by HMSO and available at most booksellers. It is a guide to modern driving techniques, produced by the Department of Transport.

Provisional licence

If you have never driven before you will need to apply for a provisional driving licence. The application form is available from post offices and it is called a D1. You must be over 17 years old unless you are applying to drive an invalid carriage, moped or some sort of farm vehicle (in which case you can apply at 16). The application form asks a variety of questions about yourself: what kind of licence you require; details of your previous licence if you had one; whether you have ever been convicted of any driving offences or been disqualified; together with details about your health – particularly your eyesight. The current fee for a provisional licence is £10. The completed form and the fee must be returned to DVLC and you may not begin driving until you are in possession of your driving licence – so apply in plenty of time. It usually takes at least three weeks, and if you have any medical conditions it may take longer.

When you receive your provisional driving licence you will also be sent a booklet called *Your Driving Test* produced by the Department of Transport. This booklet contains a lot of useful information including how to prepare for the test and apply for it.

Your provisional licence will be valid until you reach the age of 70. The only exceptions to this are if you apply for your driving licence after the age of 67 or if you have certain medical conditions, in which case you may be given a licence which will last for one to three years and will be renewable, free of charge, provided your health does not deteriorate.

At all times whilst driving on a provisional licence you must display 'L' plates, which must be clearly visible from the back and the front of the vehicle and must be securely fixed. The letter must be red on a white background. You can buy stick-on ones relatively cheaply from most garages and these are probably the best kind because they fix on securely, although they may be a bit difficult to get off and may damage the paintwork. Failure to display both 'L' plates (back and front) is an offence – even if you do not know that you have lost one. The 'L' plates should be removed when the vehicle is being driven by a qualified driver. You must always be accompanied by a fully qualified driver who holds a current British licence, and you must not drive on a motorway. There are other restrictions on learner drivers which are fully detailed in the highway code.

A learner driver is expected to obey all motoring rules and regulations. The qualified driver who accompanies a learner must supervise at all times and this must be from inside the car. It is an offence to give instruction from outside the vehicle. The supervisor must sit in the front passenger seat of the car in order to be able to take some limited action if anything goes wrong and must be attentive at all times when the car is being driven. If the supervisor dozes off or sits in the back of the car, an offence may be committed.

Anybody supervising a learner driver has to take full responsibility for the learner and must ensure that the learner does not drive in a careless or dangerous way. If the supervisor fails in this duty and an accident results, and if the learner is charged with careless driving, the person supervising may be charged with aiding and abetting the offence.

Finding an instructor

All professional driving instructors must be approved by the Department of Transport and will need to have passed an examination. Under the terms of the Road Traffic Act 1972 it is the instructor, not the school, who has to be registered. Any instructor charging for lessons who is not so approved will be committing an offence.

The Department of Transport has a register of approved driving instructors. The address is on page 233.

Since June 1986 registered driving instructors are required by law to display their licence on the vehicle. The front of the licence will have a photograph of the approved driving instructor together with the name and number. It must also show the name and address of the training establishment for which the licence is valid and the dates of issue and expiry. The licence will be either triangular in shape and pink in colour, with the wording 'Licensed Trainee Driving Instructor' on the back, or, if the instructor is qualified, it will be octagonal and green with the wording 'Department of Transport Approved Driving Instructor' on the back.

There is a trade association called the Motor Schools Association of Great Britain, whose address is on page 233. This organisation represents a large number of driving instructors who, in addition to being approved instructors, must comply with a code of conduct drawn up between the trade association and the Office of Fair Trading. If you have a complaint about an instructor who is one of their members they will take up your complaint providing you give details in writing. They are also able to supply names and addresses of local members and will give information and advice on all sorts of matters concerning driving and road safety.

The Royal Automobile Club (RAC), whose address is on page 233, maintains a register of RAC registered instructors. These instructors must have passed a further examination as well as being Department of Transport approved. If a school wishes to be part of the scheme it must employ over 50 per cent of RAC registered instructors. The RAC will supply addresses of local RAC Department of Transport registered schools and instructors, and will also take up complaints against their registered instructors. The RAC also supplies some useful publications including *Car Driving for Beginners* and *The Complete Learner Driver*.

How much to pay

It is in your own interest to find the very best instructor when you are learning to drive. However, you should also shop around for the best deal. Before employing a driving instructor, obtain quotes from as many driving schools as possible in your area. The cost of driving lessons varies around the country and from school to school.

The Motor Schools Association of Great Britain carried out a survey of lesson prices. The survey revealed that the average national price for lessons is £8.60 for one hour. Prices varied enormously across the country and the highest and lowest prices were both found in London where the lowest was £4.20 and the highest £22.

Of course, as with everything, cheapest is not always best and if a driving school is run well, their overheads can be quite high. For example it is important that their cars are well maintained at all times; they should have adequate documentation and appointments systems; instructors must keep up to date with changes in legislation, driving regulations and teaching methods and therefore they should be prepared to attend re-training courses when necessary, and these can be expensive. In addition, if the school is a particularly large school, as well as the overheads of running an office, the school may need to register for VAT and this may add to the cost of the lesson.

Many schools may offer a discount for lessons paid in advance. Whilst this can save you money, it may not be the best thing to do right at the beginning. For example, you may have paid for six lessons with a particular instructor and then find that you are not happy with the instructor. If you cancel the arrangement once you have committed yourself, you are going to lose money. The best advice would probably be to try to find an instructor who is a member of the Motor Schools Association. Members should display the Association's badge on the car (see page 233).

If you are unable to find a local member then you would be wise to take a trial lesson or several trial lessons. You should talk to the instructor after the first lesson to discuss your future programme. Some schools offer an assessment lesson after which they will be able to advise you how many lessons you are likely to need. The value of such an assessment is questionable because during the first lesson, you will be learning the very basics of how to operate the car and it would be very difficult for an instructor to be able to tell at the end of that lesson what kind of road sense you have and what your ability is likely to be. It is really not until after the fourth or fifth lesson that a proper assessment can be done, especially if you are a real novice who may be very bright and keen but have not had any road experience. You may not even have ridden a bike or have travelled very much in cars and so your road sense will be limited.

Some large, multi-car schools (more than 10 cars) may still offer lessons on credit. You may not be able to find many schools who still do so because anyone involved in credit must have a consumer credit licence which is issued by the Office of Fair Trading and the licence has to be paid for. This means the cost will be passed on and so often the interest rates on such agreements are very high.

If you can still find a driving school which offers a credit agreement for payment of the lessons then check very carefully whether it is going to be worth your while before you sign anything. You should find out what the cash price of the lessons will be, check the total amount of interest you are going to have to pay and the total overall cost. If the total cost is going to be greatly in excess of the cash price and if you really cannot afford to meet the cost on a lesson-by-lesson basis, then you may like to consider obtaining a loan from a cheaper source – eg a bank loan, and if the driving school offers discounts for payments in advance you may almost be able to break even by making that kind of arrangement.

Method of teaching

Standards of teaching vary from school to school and instructor to instructor. The examinations which instructors have to pass are based on their driving ability and their ability to *instruct* not *teach* and they receive no test of their ability to run a business.

It is relatively cheap to set yourself up as a driving instructor. Once you have got the car, you can take a course, pass your exams and set yourself up in business for about £1,000. Therefore, this may be considered quite a good bet for somebody who has been made redundant and wishes to use their redundancy pay to set themselves up in business. Such an individual could turn out to be a wonderful instructor and an equally good businessman. However, there is no guarantee and it is advisable to try different instructors until you find one in whom you have confidence and who is able to offer you a clearly defined programme. You need to have confidence in your instructor but you also need to know how you are getting along.

A really good school should have a syllabus and you could ask for a copy. You should be given regular progress reports and, because driving instructors are aware that some people may have difficulty meeting the cost of lessons, they may tell you when you are ready to go out with a supervisor (a friend or relative who is a qualified driver). Your instructor should be prepared to have a chat with the person who is going to supervise you and to tell you both what points you need to practise. For example, you may need to practise approaching roundabouts or reversing and so on.

A good instructor should take you through a mock test about four or five lessons before your test. If necessary, the instructor should take you through several mock tests. If you are taking lessons with a large school, your instructor may be able to arrange for you to take the mock test with a different instructor who could simulate test conditions. Thus giving you a real feel of what it will be like to take the test with a complete stranger.

Number of lessons

The number of lessons you are likely to need will, of course, be totally dependent on your own ability. As we get older our ability to learn new things decreases. It used to be said that people would need one lesson for every year of their life if they were under 40 and one and a half lessons for every year if they were over 40. These days, the number of lessons has increased because traffic conditions have changed so enormously and there is a lot more to learn. Generally, you should need two lessons for every year of your life under 40 and two and a half to three lessons for every year of your life over 40, but this is only a very rough guide in order to give you some idea of the total number of lessons you should require and what the whole course is likely to cost you.

Things to look out for

One of the most common complaints about driving instructors is that of broken appointments and whether or not you will still be charged. If the school offers a good appointment system there really should not be any problems, but sometimes you may need to cancel or change a lesson at fairly short notice and if the school does not have a good system, mix-ups can cost you money. In effect, if you cancel an appointment you will be in breach of contract and the school would be entitled to charge you for that lesson. However, most schools will have conditions which should be shown on your appointment card. The conditions may allow for cancellations without penalty in certain circumstances. For example, they may say that if you cancel giving 24 hours' notice you will not have to pay the cost of the lesson. Problems may arise when you have paid in advance and where the school has not correctly recorded your cancellation. Check carefully the kind of conditions imposed by the school you are using. You are expected to read the terms of any contract which you enter into and be bound by those terms and conditions.

Beware of any contract which commits you to a minimum number of lessons. If you make such a contract and then decide that you wish to cancel it halfway through the course of lessons, you may still be liable for the full cost of the course.

You need to check things like whether the instructor will collect you from your home and return you at the end of the lesson; whether the school will supply a substitute instructor if yours is taken ill or is unavailable for some other reason; and you could also check whether the school offers deferred payment terms as many do these days.

Collection

Some of the very large schools (eg British School of Motoring) always used to expect you to present yourself at their local office for your lesson. These days many of them will arrange to collect you from your home or place of work or wherever is convenient. If it is important to you that a collection service is offered then make sure you check this with the school before you book any course of lessons. You should also check whether or not this will either add to the cost or reduce the time you will get in your lesson.

Generally, a driving lesson is an hour although some schools arrange for lessons of 45 or 50 minutes. You should make sure that you are getting the full amount of time for which you are paying. For example, you should make sure that your instructor is not giving you short time by doing a few personal chores during your lesson, such as popping into the bank or picking up bits of shopping. If instructors do take time out of your lesson for their own personal business, you should complain about it at the time and make sure that the time of your lesson is extended.

Piggy-backing

Piggy-backing is the name given to the practice of picking up another learner driver for his or her next lesson, during your lesson.

There are mixed views about whether or not this practice is acceptable. Some say that it is quite useful for both of the learner drivers because it helps to give them confidence.

If your instructor does pick up another learner and you are unnerved by having a stranger in the car, then you must say so at the time and ensure that it does not happen again. It may be that if you sit in with another learner who is at a much more advanced stage than you it will, in fact, adversely affect your confidence level.

Complaints

The important thing to remember is that if your instructor does anything during the course of your lesson which you are unhappy about, you must complain at the time. Do not simply cancel your course of lessons without saying why because you may be financially penalised. In any event, the instructor should be made aware of your dissatisfaction.

Finally, if your instructor is a member of the Motor Schools Association and you are very unhappy about any of his or her practices, take your complaint to the Association who will take the matter up with the instructor.

If you are dissatisfied with your instructor you must notify the school immediately, in writing, and keep a copy of your letter. You should ask the school to supply you with another instructor or, if it is unable or unwilling to do so, you should insist upon a refund of any money you have already paid towards future lessons.

Insurance

Driving instructors must have adequate insurance to cover you while you are driving their vehicles and if you are worried about this ask to see a copy of the policy. It is *your* responsibility to make sure that the insurance cover is adequate. If it is not adequate, it is you that will be prosecuted and the instructor will be prosecuted for aiding and abetting. You would, however, have a civil claim against your driving instructor and could sue him or her for damages.

Preparing for the test

Your driving instructor will advise you when he or she thinks you are ready to take your driving test. Do not apply too soon as this will just be a waste of your money. In most cases your instructor will apply for you, but if not, you can obtain an application form (DL26) from a post office or traffic area office. The address of your local traffic area office can be found in the telephone directory under 'Transport, Department of'. If you are a disabled driver or if you are deaf and dumb, attach a note with the application form to this effect

and you will be given priority. After your application, you will
receive a card telling you where and when you will be tested. Usually
the card will arrive within 21 days of your application. If the date,
time and place are not convenient you must notify the traffic area
office immediately and return your appointment card. You must
give them at least three days' notice otherwise you will be expeced to
make a further application and you will have to pay the fee again.

If you are deaf and dumb or if you do not speak or understand
English very well you will be allowed to bring an interpreter with
you. The interpreter must not, however, be your instructor.

There are no clear statistics regarding how many people pass their
driving test at the first attempt, although the driving school which
you select will no doubt have their own details of pass rates. You
should ask about their pass rate because it says something about the
quality of instruction.

The national pass rate in 1985 was 49 per cent. The number of
people taking the driving test in that year was 1.9 million. A survey
revealed that 93 per cent of people taking a driving test had *some*
contact with a driving school. This does not necessarily mean that
they had had a whole course of lessons, and in some cases, they may
not have had enough lessons – perhaps because they could not afford
a full course.

You are much more likely to pass your driving test if you have been
able to attend a full course of instruction with a qualified driving
instructor. You should not have picked up any bad habits and you
should have been carefully prepared for the test.

Taking the test

On the day of your test make certian that: your vehicle is in a
roadworthy condition; if you need glasses or contact lenses, that you
are wearing them; 'L' plates are fitted to the vehicle; and that you
arrive at the test centre in plenty of time. It may be difficult to park
and if you are late and your test is cancelled, you will lose your fee.

The examiner will be looking at your ability to drive and you will not
pass your test unless you can drive safely and answer all of the
questions. Your examiner is not allowed to give you advice or help

and will not chat to you while you are driving in case you are distracted. If you make a mistake try not to dwell on it, continue to drive to the best of your ability until the end of the test.

At the end of the test the examiner will advise you whether you have passed or failed. If you have failed, he or she will not be able to discuss the details with you, but will provide you with a document called a statement of failure (form DL24) and this form will show the reasons for failure. There may also, however, have been other minor faults in your driving so you and your instructor will have to correct the main faults detailed on the form as well as trying to improve generally your standard of driving before applying for a test again. If you fail your driving test, you must wait a full month before you can be tested again.

If you pass your driving test you should apply for a full licence. You can use the licence application form (D1) and you should enclose your green pass certificate. You will not be required to pay the £10 fee again if you are simply applying for a full licence having passed your driving test.

Advanced driving

Once you have been driving for a few years and have gained some experience, you may think yourself a pretty good driver. Many people who have been on the road for 20 years or more are convinced that they are good drivers, but there is more to good driving than just never having an accident – you could just be lucky.

Really good driving is about skilful sympathetic handling of the vehicle; safety; consideration of other road users and pedestrians; adherence to speed limits, signals and markings; good observation and anticipation; a thorough knowledge of the highway code; and concentration. It is also about not developing bad driving habits which are both inconsiderate and damaging to your car and which may also be unsafe.

One way to find out whether you are as good a driver as you think you are would be to take the advanced driving test. These tests are conducted by the Institute of Advanced Motorists whose address is on page 233.

The Institute was founded in 1956 to promote road safety by improving the standard of driving, and some 171,000 motorists have passed the advanced test.

The IAM tests about 10,000 drivers a year and it is estimated that between 70 and 80 per cent of applicants are successful, usually because they have been carefully prepared for the test by a member.

If you write to the Institute of Advanced Motorists they will send you details of the membership and a test application form, together with a list of local groups. There are about 170 of these voluntary groups around the country whose members are able to coach people free of charge.

It is possible to take the test without any preparation but you should at least talk to a local member and ask him or her to observe your driving. They would then be able to advise and make recommendations regarding any points you may need to brush up on. In any case, you should refresh your memory of the highway code and you could also read the IAM's own manual entitled *Advanced Motoring* or the police drivers' textbook *Roadcraft*. Both are available from bookshops. If you want more detailed instruction before applying for the advanced test, some driving schools offer this, but you should ensure that the instructor is an advanced driver. In addition, some local authorities run advanced driving courses and you could find out more about them by contacting your local council's road safety officer.

The Institute has over 160 examiners all of whom hold the Police Advanced Driving Certificate. These examiners are appointed not just for their high qualification but also for their communication skills.

Applying for the test is just a matter of completing a form. The fee for application is £24 – this consists of £16.50 test fee plus £7.50 for the first year of membership to the Institute (the £7.50 is refundable if you fail).

The test itself lasts about 90 minutes and covers 35–40 miles. The route will incorporate a variety of road conditions, such as country lanes, residential areas, congested urban areas, main roads and motorways.

You are not required to give a running commentary but the examiner will make a few spot checks to test your powers of observation. The examiner will be looking for progressive, safe, higher-than-average driving skills, and at the end of the test you will be given a personal debriefing and told whether or not you have been successful. If you have not been successful you will be told why. There are a number of things which would fail you – incorrect assessment of hazards, bad use of gears, bad positioning, late or harsh braking and poor distance observation are some of the most common mistakes made by even the most experienced of drivers.

If you pass the test, you will become a member of the Institute of Advanced Motorists and as such will be entitled to display the Institute's badge (see page 233) on your car to show that you are an advanced motorist. You will then be expected to set an example to other drivers.

Statistically, advanced motorists are 50–75 per cent less likely to be involved in an accident than the average driver. This fact is recognised by some insurance companies who will offer up to 20 per cent discount on insurance premiums to advanced motorists, and those kinds of savings are worth taking advantage of when you consider the overall costs of running a car these days.

Buying a car

New cars

After your house, a car is probably the most expensive purchase you are likely to make and it is very easy to be swayed by the appearance of a vehicle, advertising or a salesperson.

Approximately 1.7 million new cars are purchased every year. However, about 60 per cent of those are purchased by trade or industry. Roughly two out of three motorists buy secondhand – even people who could actually afford to buy new may choose to purchase a car which is about a year old. This is because buying a new car is not always cost effective or even convenient.

New cars have to be properly run in. They must be serviced at the correct intervals and all too many new cars experience 'teething troubles'. After about a year, all of these problems should have been overcome and the car will have devalued considerably. A new car will lose about a third of its value in its first two years and about half its value within three years. A car loses several hundred pounds as soon as it is put on the road. This means that for many people, buying a car which is maybe one or two years old is a much better idea than buying a brand new one. Once you have decided that you are going to buy new then since this is such a major investment you should be quite certain of what you want before you go shopping.

It has been said that you should never go to the supermarket for the weekly shopping on an empty stomach. This is because you are much more likely to buy all sorts of foods that take your fancy because you are hungry rather than the things that you really need. The message here is to plan your car purchase well in advance. Do not go to a showroom without any idea of what you want or when you need a car in a hurry.

The best way to ensure that you do not make a very expensive mistake is to prepare a checklist. Your checklist could have seven main headings:

- cost
- running costs
- convenience
- comfort
- noise
- size
- colour

Cost

Obviously how much you pay is going to be a very important factor so you need to make a decision about the maximum price you can afford before you go shopping. Whether you are paying cash or buying on credit you should shop around the franchised dealers. Many of them will give excellent discounts and these discounts can be better at certain times of the year. Vehicles are registered on 1 August (although this is likely to change to October). When cars are about to receive their new registration letters everybody tends to wait for the new letter before buying. If this is not particularly important to you, then you may be able to make big savings by buying a car which has already been registered by the dealer. These are often called demonstration cars and will be sold off at very good prices. Remember that the bigger the dealer the bigger the discount you are likely to get. The car dealers' margin is around 15–17.5 per cent and you may be able to get as much as that on a demonstration model. Sometimes dealers will register cars which they have in stock in order to enhance that particular year's sales figures and when the new models become available dealers will make fairly big reductions.

The time of year you buy, therefore, is very important in terms of how much you are likely to spend. There are times of the year when dealers find 'shifting the metal', as it is known in the trade, more difficult than others. For example, car showrooms are pretty deserted in December and for a short while after Christmas. Plenty of people want to sell cars but very few are interested in buying and so dealers will offer good reductions at this time. In July when people are more interested in spending their hard-earned cash on a holiday than buying a new car, especially if they are waiting for the new registration letter, dealers will again be offering excellent discounts on the old registration letter.

You should also consider whether or not it is in your best interests to trade-in another car. Only one in ten car sales these days do not involve trade-ins, although it may be more cost-effective for you to consider selling your old car privately and therefore getting a better price than part exchanging it for a new one, particularly if this means that you will be able to pay cash for the new car. In this case, of course, you should seek an additional discount for cash.

Running costs

The running costs of your car are going to be a major consideration. The initial expenditure is one thing but some cars can be a lot more expensive to run than others. Under this heading you need to consider the obvious things like petrol consumption, the cost of parts and so on, but also the less obvious things like how much it is going to cost you to insure it. Find out which group the car falls into in insurance terms, because obviously a group 7 car is going to be considerably more expensive to insure than a group 1. You must also consider servicing costs. For example, some cars need to be serviced every 3,000 miles whilst others need servicing only every 6,000 miles. Apart from the time between servicing you should also consider the cost of parts and how easy (or not) it is to get those parts and also labour costs. Labour charges vary enormously around the country and from garage to garage. It is true to say that a garage which specialises in certain makes of car can carry out repairs more quickly and therefore save you on labour charges. However, some cars may be more difficult to service than others. A replacement clutch, for example, may involve two to three hours' labour on one model of car and up to eleven hours' labour on another. With labour charges hovering at around £18 an hour in some areas this can mean the difference of £140 on one repair.

Convenience

The question of how convenient your car is going to be relates to some of the things that we have already mentioned. For example, is it likely to be off the road for a long time while the dealer obtains parts for you, or because repairs take a long time? Another consideration is whether or not you have a franchised dealer nearby. In some parts of the country you may have to travel quite a long way to find your nearest specialist in that particular car. Apart from the cost implications (petrol, wear and tear, etc) there is also the difficulty of travelling to and from the dealer by some other method when you take the car in for a service.

Other considerations may be special to your particular needs, such as luggage space; whether or not the car is capable of towing a caravan or trailer should you need to; the ease of fitting a roof rack; whether you need two, four or five doors; whether you need an estate; if the glove compartment is big enough; whether the shelves or other storage areas are large enough and accessible; and so on.

Are all the controls within easy reach, clearly visible and safe? Research has shown that certain types of controls, for example those which are not flush with the dashboard, have been known to cause serious injuries in the event of an accident.

Comfort

Comfort is extremely important particularly to the driver. This is something that you will really only be able to assess by trying out various cars. The height and adjustability of the driving seat is important, and its position in relation to the steering wheel and gear lever should be comfortable. Uncomfortable gear changes can have a bad effect on your health and therefore your concentration if you have to drive in heavy traffic regularly. The controls should be reached with comfort and convenience. The seat belts must also be comfortable – some seat belts tend to be fixed fairly high up or far back (especially on two door cars) and this means that for some people they will cut into the side of the neck, or at any rate be very uncomfortable. Check the vision all around the car. Many cars have blind spots but some are far worse than others and good interior vision is important to good driving. Is there enough space in the back of the car for the children or the family pet? Are there rear seat belts? And if you are going to need to fix harnesses or safety seats for children, will they be easy to fit?

Noise

Noise is another very important consideration. Some cars, especially the smaller cars, can be extremely noisy if travelling at relatively high speeds, for example on a motorway, making conversation almost impossible. If you are going to be using your car on a lot of relatively long journeys this could be an important consideration.

Size

The size of the car is another important consideration; not just the amount of space that you have inside the vehicle, which we have already looked at, but its overall dimensions. It is no good buying a beautiful estate and then finding that it will not fit into your garage or parking space; and remember that parking is a major consideration not just at home but all the time. Is the car easy to handle in terms of its size and are you going to find it difficult to park?

The size of your car can affect costs in other ways too. For instance, if you travel abroad, or even just over to the Isle of Wight, the cost of taking your car onto a ferry goes up with the length of the car.

Colour

This may sound like a relatively unimportant consideration but it is amazing how many people are persuaded to buy a car because of its colour.

Many years ago Henry Ford was reported as saying 'you can have any colour you like as long as it's black'. This, of course, is no longer true and cars come in an enormous variety of colours and types of paintwork.

However, there is still a great deal to be said for having a black car. Apart from the fact that they have now become trendy and sporty looking again, it is easy to match up black paint whenever you have minor cosmetic repairs to do. Other colours are not so easy and certain types of paintwork (eg metallic) can be very difficult to match and very quickly lose their showroom gloss. One of the most difficult colours to match is white. There are huge variations in whites: there are creamy whites, bluey whites and so on, but even if you manage to get exactly the same paint which was used in the original manufacture, white cars fade very quickly particularly when they are used in heavy traffic, not garaged or exposed to bright sunlight or other extreme weather conditions.

Red cars continue to maintain their popularity because of their sporty appearance but they can be a disadvantage in that they get noticed – in more ways than one! A young, or young-looking, driver in a flashy car is likely to be stopped more frequently by the police for document checks. Equally, it is generally assumed that a driver who favours a flashy-looking car favours high-speed driving!

Being noticed, however, is not always a disadvantage. I once owned a car which was a grey-blue colour and it seemed that every time I left it somewhere somebody hit it. During one of its many trips to the garage for cosmetic repairs, the dealer told me that it was very common for grey and grey-blue cars to sustain more damage than any other colour. This is because they are less easy to see, particularly at certain times of the day, such as dusk, or in very bad weather conditions, like heavy rain or fog.

Extras

When buying your new car be wary of additional costs which you may not have considered as 'extras'. Some manufacturers add on a 'delivery charge'. You may also find a charge for number plates, undersealing, as well as radio/cassette player and aerial. There may also be an additional charge for an extended warranty.

Some of the extras which you may want on the car could be cheaper to have fitted when you buy the car rather than having them fitted later – particularly items such as the radio, aerial, additional seat belts, cigar lighter and so on.

Where to buy

The next step is to select your dealer. Choose a large reputable franchised dealer who has been around for a long time.

When you buy goods of any kind you have protection in law. In the case of a new or used car you will have additional protection if you go to a dealer which is a member of one of the trade associations. This is because there is a code of practice which has been drawn up by the trade in conjunction with the Office of Fair Trading and all members of the relevant trade associations must adhere to the terms of the code. The trade associations concerned are the Motor Agents Association Ltd, Society of Motor Manufacturers & Traders Ltd, Scottish Motor Trade Association Ltd and Vehicle Builders and Repairers Association – all addresses are listed on page 233.

A free leaflet entitled *Cars* which sets out the details of the code of practice is available from the Office of Fair Trading or your local consumer advice centre, Citizens Advice Bureau or Trading Standards Department. The first three trade associations have a code which is specifically for the motor industry and the last one has a code which deals only with vehicle body repairs for cars and caravans.

If the dealer you select is a member of one of the trade associations it should display the relevant logos (see pages 233).

You can contact the associations for lists of local members or if you are in doubt about a local dealer's membership. A dealer will be committing an offence under the Trade Descriptions Act if a logo of a trade association is displayed and the dealer is not currently a member.

Dealers who are members and abide by the code of practice must ensure that a pre-delivery inspection is carried out correctly and that you are given a copy of the checklist; they must also ensure that you are fully aware of the main provisions of the manufacturer's warranty; they must give you the handbook at the time of the sale; and they must show the total cost of putting the car on the road on your order form.

Warranties and guarantees

Like a code of practice, a warranty or guarantee can only give you rights over and above those which you already have in law.

If a warranty is free then you may just as well have it. However, if you are going to have to pay for an extended warranty then you need to check whether or not it is really worth having.

In most cases, a warranty imposes a variety of conditions which must be strictly adhered to otherwise the warranty will be invalidated. These conditions include things like ensuring that the manufacturer's recommended servicing instructions are adhered to – specifically the length of time between servicing, and who does the repairs, and there may also be conditions regarding how the warranty company is notified of any claim you may wish to make. Conditions like this can cause delays and in fact they usually do. It can mean that your car may be off the road for some time or it can mean that the warranty company will not meet your claim if you have not followed their instructions to the letter. You may be better off investing the cost of any extended warranty because it is after all a form of insurance. If you have a claim, well you will have some money there towards the cost, and if you do not have a claim you will still have your money.

Warranties, however, can never take away your statutory rights. These rights are spelt out in the Sale of Goods Act 1979. This law says that goods which you buy must be of merchantable quality, fit for the purpose and as described, and if goods are not all of those things then you are entitled to reject them and ask for your money back. For more details on warranties and on your rights see chapter 7.

Ordering and taking delivery

If the car has to be ordered, check the clauses in the contract very carefully, particularly those clauses which may relate to delay if the car is not ready when you need it. Certain cars may be more difficult to get than others and there may be quite a long wait. This may affect the delivery price which can increase between the time when you ordered the car and the time when you finally take delivery of it. In most cases, contracts will have a clause which gives you an option of withdrawing from the purchase if such an increase has taken place.

Make sure if you are ordering a car that any extras which you have ordered are clearly shown on the contract and that any other special instructions are written down. Do not sign anything unless you fully understand it and are completely happy about the terms.

When your car is ready, examine it very carefully in the showroom for cosmetic faults. Take it for a test drive and if there are any minor adjustments necessary before you finally take delivery, make sure that these are done before you accept it and examine it once again before you take it away.

Importing

It has, for some time, been possible to buy cars on the continent and import them into this country at a considerable saving. There are several reasons why cars may be cheaper if bought outside the UK.

Why import?

The major reason is the 10 per cent tax which is imposed in this country on all new cars – and this is *before* VAT. In some European countries, far from additional taxation, government subsidies operate in order to boost sales.

In addition, fluctuations in exchange rates mean that buying abroad can effect even greater savings if you buy at the right time. These fluctuations, however, can also adversely affect the importation of foreign cars into this country by the trade, because the car tax is percentage-based. This means that buying a foreign car in this country at the wrong time will mean paying an inflated price for it.

One of the other factors which influences the cost of foreign imports is the expectations of consumers and the standards which exist. European car owners have different requirements and in many cases, accept far lower manufacturing specifications than we do. This is because there is nothing like the same secondhand market in Europe as there is in Britain. Trade-ins are much less common and so dealers keep new car prices down in order to attract custom.

A good example of the different expectations of European and British consumers is the Mercedes. We consider it a luxury car and therefore expect high standards of manufacture and plenty of 'extras' – for which we are prepared to pay. However, in Belgium, Mercedes are used as taxis and so can be bought relatively cheaply, although they would be fairly basic models produced to a standard unacceptable to most British consumers.

Even taking account of the duty which will have to be paid on a car imported for personal use, great savings can be achieved and it may be worth considering if you are prepared to go to the trouble of organising it.

How to import

If you cannot cope with doing it yourself but want to take advantage of the chance to save money, there are dealers who will do it for you. But beware! At least three such dealers went bust in 1985. Also, many people have experienced all sorts of problems, including lengthy delays, cars which were not as specified, price increases, etc – some of which were exacerbated by import delays. Lack of communication and having to pay large deposits in advance have also been the cause of many complaints.

Consumers' Association, the publishers of *Which?* magazine, have produced an action kit called *Importing a Car* and this is available direct from them. If you are considering importing a car it is worth investing in the kit.

An EEC regulation (123/85) came into effect in July 1985 and this regulation made it easier for consumers buying abroad to obtain lower prices. Cars manufactured with left-hand drive should not cost any more to be converted to right-hand drive although dealers are permitted to make charges for any differences in specifications or delivery costs.

The Department of Transport has produced a leaflet entitled *Permanent Import of Motor Vehicles into Great Britain* and the leaflet details all of the information you would need when importing whether the car is new or secondhand.

All vehicles sold in the UK have to have a National Type Approval Certificate which shows that the vehicle meets all British safety and environmental regulations. Without this certification, a new car cannot be licensed. There are certain exceptions (motor caravans and vehicles which have been brought temporarily into the country by someone who normally lives abroad). However, imported cars must comply with a variety of other requirements before you can take them on the road. For example you must have valid insurance. Usually it will be possible to obtain temporary cover through the local AA or RAC office at the port of arrival, even if you are not a member. You must have a current vehicle excise licence (road tax), and you will be given the relevant application form after the vehicle has been cleared by customs. You will be unable to tax your vehicle without this form and you will also have to show your current certificate of insurance. If the car you are importing is not a new car it may also require an MOT test certificate, and you will only be permitted to drive the car from the port of arrival to your personal destination and, by prior appointment, to the testing station. If a test certificate is refused, the situation regarding continued driving of the vehicle is the same as that following any refusal of a test certificate.

Any vehicle which has been imported must comply with the Motor Vehicles (Construction and Use) Regulations and with the Road Vehicle Lighting Regulations and also, possibly, with the Road Vehicles (Rear Fog Lamps) Regulations. One of the terms of these regulations states that certain components of certain vehicles should be marked to indicate that they have been manufactured to a prescribed standard. Generally, cars holding a National Type Approval Certificate will comply with these marking requirements or they may be exempt. However, personally imported cars are likely to need some modification in order to comply with the standards required in this country. In some cases, the relevant parts can simply be replaced, but items such as door locks and hinges, radio suppression, exhaust systems and other things which are integral or constructional may not be so easily replaceable. Although non-compliance will not prevent you from registering and licensing the vehicle, you will be committing an offence if you drive the vehicle in Britain.

You must ensure that you have British registration number plates fitted to the vehicle. These can be obtained from a local dealer as soon as the vehicle has been allocated its registration number.

Used cars

That secondhand car of your dreams may be just within your price
range but before you get behind the wheel there are all sorts of
considerations which you need to check up on before deciding which
car to buy.

For example, you are going to have to insure it, and if you are young
or have not been driving very long the cost of insurance may be more
than the price of the car.

Certain cars are often sold cheaply (eg large cars) because of their
higher running costs. This may also apply to many foreign cars and
obsolete British-made smaller cars; they will probably be cheaper to
buy but spare parts and repairs could cost much more than average.

It is estimated that roughly two million used cars are bought every
year in this country and, as we have already seen, approximately 60
per cent of new cars are purchased by businesses. These company
cars can run up very, very high mileages – sometimes as much as
30–40,000 miles a year. The average annual mileage is about 12,000
miles so you can see that buying an ex-company car may not be a
very good deal. In addition to unusually high mileage, these cars
often have not been cared for in the same way that a private owner
would look after a car.

Ex-company vehicles are very easy to come by from a dealer's point
of view (they are usually sold off at auction). There is a great
temptation for unscrupulous dealers to buy such cars and 'clock'
them. This means turning back the mileometer or, to give it it's
correct name, odometer.

Cost

The price of a used car is determined by a number of factors – the
general condition of the bodywork and engine, the current demands
for specific types of car and, in particular, the mileage. The average
motorist covers approximately 12,000 miles per year. For every
1,000 miles over the average, a dealer will deduct about £30
(although this figure varies depending on the type of vehicle, and can
be as much as £70 per 1,000 miles on a luxury car). From evidence
obtained through prosecutions, it has been shown that the average

number of miles deducted on a 'clocked' vehicle is 39,000. Thus, you can see that from a dealer's point of view this represents £1,070. The fines imposed on dealers (if they are caught) are surprisingly low – on average about £300. That, of course, is why the temptation to clock cars is so great and it has been estimated that this practice costs consumers about £100,000 a year.

How can you find out whether a car has been clocked? Probably the only sure way is to check the car's history, talk to previous owners and check the mileage recorded on old MOT certificates, but this, of course, is not always possible. That information just may not be available to you, in which case the best advice is to get the car independently examined before buying it. An experienced engineer will be able to tell whether the general overall condition of the car – the engine, interior wear and so on – is consistent with the recorded mileage. He may also be able to tell whether a clock has been tampered with or not.

In one year alone (1984), advice agencies and trading standards departments dealt with 86,472 complaints about vehicles. Many of the complaints received each year do not result in a satisfactory outcome for the consumer, and remember that these are only the *recorded* complaints. Thousands of consumers do not seek help and just put it down to experience, because the average motorist wants low-cost, reliability and safety – and usually in that order. The most common exception to that rule is the car dealer's dream. A youngster who just wants a car to impress his friends. It does not necessarily have to go like a bomb as long as it looks and sounds like it does. This buyer knows nothing about cars, has never owned one before and will not take Dad's advice. He has not bothered to check the cost of insurance and the dealer certainly is not going to say anything.

Many of the problems which occur after purchase could have been avoided by doing a little homework first. Too often, people go out to buy a used car with no real idea of what they want and so they are sweet-talked by a salesperson or swayed by things like a super stereo system, sun roof or other flashy extras. Deciding which model or models really suit your needs sounds obvious, but plenty of people end up buying a car which turns out to be too small or too big or in other ways unsuited to their needs, simply because a dealer has

USED VEHICLE PRE-SALES INSPECTION SCHEDULE (A)

(Approved checklist pursuant to Paragraphs 3.2 and 3.5 of the Code of Practice for the Motor Industry)

Motor Agents Association

Name and address (or stamp) of Garage:

Date of Inspection

Stock List No:
Make:
Model:
Registration No:
Date first registered:
Chassis No:
Engine No:
Repair Order Ref:
Recorded Mileage at date of sale:

This schedule quotes the mileage as recorded on the mileometer. We do not guarantee that this recorded mileage is accurate as indicating the previous history of the vehicle. However, to the best of our knowledge and belief the reading is CORRECT/INCORRECT*. (* delete as required)

New Owner:

THIS VEHICLE HAS BEEN CHECKED AS TO THE FOLLOWING ITEMS AND SUBJECTED TO ROAD/DYNAMOMETER TEST*
(* delete as necessary)

Column 1: ✓ Item Serviceable   X Item Unserviceable   N/A Not applicable   Column 2: R Item Rectified

	1	2			1	2
1. Headlights — dipped/main			36. Number plates			
2. Turning indicator lights			37. Bonnet Lock & Safety catch			
3. Turning indicator warning lights			38. Engine oil level			
4. Instrument panel lights			39. Brake fluid level			
5. Headlight flasher			40. Radiator coolant level			
6. Hazard warning			41. Radiator hoses & clips			
7. Cigar lighter			42. Fan belt/other drive belts			
8. Rear screen heater			43. HT suppression			
9. Clock			44. Battery level			
10. Radio/Tape player			45. Battery & earth connectors			
11. W/screen washers — (front/rear)			46. Battery security			
12. W/screen wipers — (front/rear)			47. Front wheel alignment			
13. Fuel indicator			48. Brake Pads/linings			
14. Courtesy lights			49. Wheel nuts			
15. Interior lights			50. Brake hoses			
16. Heater & Heater blower			51. Brake pipes & exterior hydraulics			
17. Horn			52. Exhaust system			
18. Parking lights front & rear			53. Suspension			
19. Side lights			54. Shock absorbers			
20. Reverse lights			55. Steering rods & linkage			
21. Number plate lights			56. Steering box			
22. Stop light			57. Gearbox/Axle levels			
23. Fog light			58. Tyre condition			
24. Window mechanism			59. Tyre pressures			
25. Seat security			60. Underbody inspection			
26. Seat belts			61. No excessive oil leaks			
27. Driving mirror			62. Anti-freeze (if applicable)			
28. Door closing			63. Tools as Listed:			
29. Door lock inside/outside			Other Items			
30. Child locks			64.			
31. Hub caps & discs			65.			
32. Boot lock			66.			
33. Spare wheel & tyre			67.			
34. Wheel brace						
35. Lifting Jack			INSPECTED BY			

The findings of the above condition report take into account the age and price (if relevant) of the used vehicle described.

I acknowledge receipt of a copy of this inspection checklist

(Signature of customer) ....   Date ....

White — to be displayed on vehicle   Blue — to be handed to customer   Pink — file copy   35 9 81

Sample used vehicle pre-sales inspection schedule.

persuaded them that it is 'better value' than the one they had in mind.

Other problems arise when people discover that perhaps the monthly repayments on the credit deal were much higher than they had anticipated or that the running costs make the whole deal uneconomical. If you have checked all of these things in advance, you will be spared a lot of anxiety later.

Running costs

Make sure you have budgeted for the running costs of your car. These are the things you need to consider:

- tax
- insurance
- monthly repayments (if bought on credit)
- repairs and servicing
- petrol consumption.

When you are looking at petrol consumption you must bear in mind that if the car is not running at its best it is likely to consume more, and if you are going to be using the car for short journeys in heavy traffic the consumption will be slightly higher still. Try to estimate your likely annual mileage. The following is a rough guide to average petrol consumption based on varied driving conditions:
A small car consumes 35–40 mpg
A medium car consumes 30–35 mpg
A large car consumes 20–30 mpg.
Having carefully prepared your checklist and done a bit of research you should end up with two or three particular cars in mind, all of which fit your needs.

Value

Having selected the type of car you want, you will need to find out the sort of price these cars are going for. You may end up buying an older model than you would have liked, especially if you have selected a car which holds its value particularly well. You can get an idea of prices by looking in the local papers and by buying motoring magazines. Prices can vary considerably according to local supply and demand, as well as the condition of the car. We have already looked at some aspects of depreciation (see page 51) but certain cars hold their value better than others. The AA suggests that cars are written off after 80,000 miles or eight years, in which case a car would depreciate by an eighth of its original cost per year.

Insurance companies and the trade generally agree that cars no longer have a 'book' value after 10 years so that pricing a car older than that would be wholly dependant upon the condition of the individual vehicle. There are, of course, exceptions where cars will sell for much more than their original, new price. Vintage cars fall into this category of course, certain custom cars and other rare models.

The reference to 'book' value comes from a publication called *Glass's Guide*. This is the car dealers' bible and it is only available to the trade. *Glass's Guide* contains details of used car values for virtually every model available in this country, including diesels. The guide shows the price new, the basic trade price (that at which the dealer would buy it) and the basic retail price (the price at which the dealer would sell it). The guide also makes allowances for mileage and as we have already said, cars with a high mileage will be a lot cheaper. The guide also contains a mileage adjustment table which deals with cars which are up to seven years old. The guide itself, however, covers a 10-year period which is one of the reasons why pricing cars older than 10 years can be so difficult. Car dealers rely on *Glass's Guide* (and a newer guide which is now available called *The Black Book*) when setting their prices but often these prices are still open to negotiation so you would be wise to be prepared for a little bargaining.

We have already said that car dealers have trouble selling new cars in December and around July, just before the new registration letters are about to come into effect. Therefore you are going to be able to get good discounts on new cars. But it should also be remembered that when you are buying a used car, this is just as good a time. Before Christmas lots of people are fairly desperate to sell their old cars because they need cash and whether you buy from a dealer or privately, this is an excellent time to pick up a real bargain. Even the auctions are pretty deserted in December.

However, if you buy a used car from a dealer in July or August any small adjustments or even fairly major repairs which may have been necessary may not have been done to the best standard. Even the pre-sale inspection may not be carried out as well as at other times. As soon as the new registration letters are issued, dealers are extremely busy and they have little interest at that time in selling used cars.

If you are going to buy privately though you may find that someone wanting to buy a new car with the new registration letter will be offering their old car for sale privately rather than as a part exchange deal. They will want to get rid of the car quickly in order to give them the capital they need for their new car and so you may be able to negotiate a much better price than that which is advertised.

If you intend to keep the car for a long time then you are going to have to pay a little more to get a newer model that is not going to need a lot of money spent on it fairly soon.

A real old banger, costing less than £500, however, could be a really good buy if you only intend keeping it for a very short time but examine it very carefully. You may be able to run it without a major repair job for a couple of years in which case you will have got your money's worth, even if it then has to be scrapped. If, on the other hand you are intending to keep the car for a long time then you must look for reliability and low depreciation so that you will not lose too much when you want to sell it.

Advertisements for bangers abound in the local papers, shop windows and even parked outside people's houses, and buying a car that may be 10 or 12 years old could be worthwhile provided it is in reasonable order. I would recommend, however, that if this is the market that you are looking at, you limit yourself to popular British cars because spare parts are in good supply and relatively cheap. It also makes good sense to avoid sports cars because they are likely to have had a bit of a beating and the insurance will be expensive.

The most important check that you need to make on a car of this age is for corrosion. Once a car of this age is suffering from extensive rust, its life is at an end.

The only way to be really sure about the condition of a car's engine is to have it independently inspected by an expert. A qualified engineer would be able to tell whether the car is as much of a bargain as you think it is.

Where to buy

You really have three choices: from a dealer; privately; at auction.

BUYING FROM A DEALER

If you buy from a dealer, find out which is the most respected local firm. This could well be your best guarantee, for a firm with a good name has a lot to lose and nothing to gain by selling an unreliable car to a local customer. If your enquiries produce no clear-cut answer, you can obtain a list of garages approved by the RAC or AA (if you are a member), or you can write to one of the trade associations to check whether a particular dealer is a member. The code of practice drawn up by the Office of Fair Trading in conjuction with the trade associations must be adhered to by member dealers. A free leaflet *Cars* outlining your rights and listing the trade associations is available from your local consumer advice centre, Citizens Advice Bureau, Trading Standards Department or from the Office of Fair Trading.

Another good source is the franchised dealers – those appointed agents by a manufacturer. Their repair facilities are usually good (though this is not to say that they always use them on secondhand cars). From time to time they sell off low-mileage demonstration models which are often excellent buys and they may also offer a fairly reasonable warranty. Buying a used car from a dealer may cost a little more but the law is tougher on dealers than it is on private individuals and so you may be buying a little extra protection.

Avoid small firms in tatty premises with no proper name displayed outside, no garage or workshop and a fairly temporary appearance. If a dealer has no repair or servicing facilities they will have done little more with the car than offer it for sale again exactly as they bought it – but with their profit margin added on.

If you do see exactly what you are looking for on show at these kinds of premises, then before even discussing the car find out exactly who you are dealing with. The Companies Act 1981 says that any business which is carried on under a name other than that of its owner, must display the details of ownership on its premises and on

all business stationery. You are also entitled to be given these
particulars, in writing, on request. For example the name outside
the premises may be 'Rippoff and Runne – Car Dealers'. If it were a
limited company (Rippoff and Runne Limited) then it must be
registered at Companies House where you could find the names and
addresses of the directors of the company, inspect the company's
annual accounts and so on. If a limited company is not registered at
Companies House or has not filed accounts for more than a year,
take your business elsewhere and advise your local Trading
Standards Department because the trader will be committing a
criminal offence. However, if it is not a limited company no such
records will exist. The only way to find out who is the proprietor of
the business is by information displayed within the premises or on
the stationery. If a trader refuses to supply it to you in writing,
report them to your local Trading Standards Department. The
information displayed, and which they are obliged to provide on
request, must include the proprietor's name and an address in the
UK which does not necessarily have to be his personal address but it
must be one where documents could be served if necessary.

Even if the trader is prepared to supply this information to you in
writing but does not have it displayed in the premises or on
stationery, such as receipts, invoices and so on, either take your
business elsewhere or take a risk that they may not be around when
your car breaks down.

Earlier I touched on the extra protection the law provides when you
buy from a dealer. The basis of this protection is the Sale of Goods
Act 1979 which says that goods which you buy (whether they are
new or secondhand) must be of merchantable quality, fit for the
purpose and as described. If you buy a car from a dealer which is not
all of those things, then you will have a civil claim for redress and if
necessary you could pursue your claim through the county court.
You would be claiming either a full refund or damages
(compensation). In addition, when buying from a dealer, there is the
Trade Descriptions Act 1968 which protects buyers from false or
misleading descriptions either spoken or in writing and a dealer who
applies a false description is guilty of a criminal offence. The
problem is obtaining proof, and smart dealers say little and put less
in writing.

The onus is very much on the buyer to ask the right questions and have a witness to the answers – or better still get something in writing. That way, if a dealer has misrepresented the car, you will have a better chance of having them prosecuted.

Conviction of a criminal offence, however, may cost the dealer a fine but it will not automatically solve your problem – namely that you have a duff car. It may be quite a long time before the criminal case comes to court and even when it does, magistrates do not award compensation to the buyer as a matter of course. Even when it *is* applied for, the award may be far less than the loss you have sustained. More details of how to obtain redress appear in chapter 7.

If you are buying from a dealer and you are not in a position to pay cash, the dealer may be able to arrange credit for you and this in itself would afford you even more protection under the terms of the Consumer Credit Act 1974. This law says that if the dealer arranges the credit for you, in other words, introduces you to the source of credit, and all of the transaction takes place at his premises, the supplier of the credit (the finance company) has to accept equal liability with the trader if anything goes wrong.

The real advantage of this legislation is that whilst a dealer may fob you off or even disappear when you have a complaint, a reputable finance company is much more likely to help you sort out your problem. This is because anybody involved in credit (finance companies, finance brokers or even car dealers who arrange credit) must be licensed by the Office of Fair Trading, and if they misbehave their licence could be revoked. As far as a car dealer is concerned, losing his consumer credit licence is really not the end of the world. It simply means that all his future business will have to be conducted on a cash basis. But if a finance company loses its consumer credit licence, it is no longer able to trade.

One final word of caution, beware of what is known as 'disguised business sales'. The Business Advertisements Disclosure Order 1977 makes it an offence for dealers to advertise vehicles in classified advertisements without making it clear that they are traders. Dishonest traders sometimes advertise from a private address or telephone number in order to evade their legal responsibilities. As we have already said, the law is much tougher on dealers than it is on private individuals and this is why tricky dealers will pretend not to be dealers at all.

Many local Trading Standards Departments monitor newspaper advertisements by checking how often the same telephone number appears in used-car advertisements. You can do the same. And if you spot the same telephone number several times in advertisements for different vehicles, report it to your local Trading Standards Officer. If the seller turns out to be a dealer working from home and masquerading as a private seller he is committing a criminal offence and could be prosecuted.

BUYING PRIVATELY

If you buy privately, you should get your car a bit cheaper because you are bypassing the dealer's profit; but there will be no guarantee, no possibility of credit and the chances are that the car has had no mechanical check up before being advertised for sale. Try to find out why the seller is disposing of the car and how long he or she has had it.

When buying privately find out as much as possible about the person who is selling the car. There have been cases where dealers, posing as private sellers, agree to meet the unsuspecting buyer to show them the car. When the buyer arrives the seller is just coming down the garden path and the car is parked outside. All of the business takes place in the car or in the street outside what the buyer assumes is the seller's house. Later, when problems develop and the buyer returns to the address, the person who lives there knows nothing of the seller or of the car! The moral here is do not ever do the business in the street. Go inside the house while the seller writes out the receipt and hands you the log book (registration document) and MOT certificate (if applicable).

If any private seller offers to bring the car to you, be cautious. It could be a stolen vehicle which you would not be able to keep and you would never be able to trace the seller again. It is very easy for people to give a false name and address so make sure that anyone selling you a car privately not only gives you a detailed receipt which contains the seller's name, address, the date, full details of the vehicle and the amount paid and is signed by the seller, but also shows you some form of identification.

Make sure that you inspect the registration document before you hand over any money and do not settle for excuses like 'it's at DVLC, I'll let you have it later'. See it before you buy and if the registered keeper shown on the registration document is not the same as the person selling the car, find out why.

The registration document will tell you how long the present keeper has had the vehicle and the number of former keepers. It will also confirm that the car you are buying is correctly described – the date of first registration and whether or not the car has been imported and manufactured before the date of first registration in this country. Cars are often described in advertisements using the registration letter. Cars are valued on their age. The letter of the registration may be misleading; for example (V) could be 1979 or 1980. It will certainly be misleading if the car has been re-registered in this country.

Before you finalise the deal, it may be worthwhile taking the name and address of the previous keeper and contacting them for some more information about its previous history, particularly its mileage. This would be especially useful if the present seller had not had the car for very long.

If the car is more than three years old it must have a valid MOT certificate. Make sure you examine the certificate and, again, look at the mileage. Do not forget that the MOT is no guarantee of the car's mechanical condition and that is clearly stated on the MOT certificate.

Always make sure that you check the documents before you hand over any money and that they are all in order. Never buy a car if the documents are not available.

If a seller tells you that they have had certain repairs done on the car then ask to see the receipts. If the car is only a few years old, the seller may have the service book. Check to see whether it has been regularly serviced and when the last service was carried out. Ask the seller whether the vehicle has had any major repairs or been involved in a serious accident.

When buying privately you should always take a witness with you. Better still, get anything which is said about the car written down at the time. You do not have the Sale of Goods Act to protect you and the only way you could take action if something goes wrong is if you can prove that the seller misrepresented the car (told you something about it which was untrue and which he knew to be untrue at the time).

The only other legal protection you have, apart from the straight forward law of contract, is the Road Traffic Act 1972 which makes it a criminal offence for anyone (a private individual or a trader) to sell a car which is clearly unroadworthy. The only exception to this would be if the seller made it clear that the car was not suitable for use on the roads (eg that it was being sold for parts or scrap). If the car is unroadworthy, and generally this means that it is in a dangerous condition, you should advise your local Trading Standards Department or the police and the seller could be prosecuted and fined. As with other criminal convictions, however, this would not guarantee you compensation but you could still sue the seller for breach of contract.

If you buy privately, your rights are very limited. The basic principle is *buyer beware*. It is your responsibility to check the car thoroughly and satisfy yourself that all is well. In essence, the only real claims you will have against a private seller will be if:

- there is a specific breach of contract, that is if the seller fails to comply with what was agreed;

- the car is not as it was described to you;

- there is a specific misrepresentation by the seller which you can prove;

- the car was completely unroadworthy, for example dangerous.

BUYING AT AUCTION

If you are brave, you may feel like bidding at a car auction. Anyone can do so, but auctions are the almost exclusive preserve of the trade and you may well find yourself the only private buyer present. Since any car bought at an auction by a dealer will obviously be resold at a higher price, you may think that this is a good way to get a bargain and bypass the middle man's profit.

It is also a good way to get cheated and as a private buyer you will be at greatest risk. Another snag is that most cars sold this way will need money spending on them and dealers who buy them are likely to be able to carry out repairs much more cheaply through their own servicing and repair facilities than you can. Also, if 30 hardened dealers are not prepared to outbid you, it could be because they know something you do not!

If you do decide to attend an auction, you can have a look at the cars beforehand although you are unlikely to be able to road test any of them. After the sale you have only 24 hours to lodge any complaint with the auctioneer, and the complaint can be sustained only if you can show that the seller's description of the condition or the age of the vehicle was false, or that it is still under a hire purchase agreement.

When you buy at an auction, the seller of the car is *not* the auctioneer. You as a buyer, have no contract with the auctioneer who is acting as an agent for the seller. The seller does have a contract with the auctioneer but that does not concern you. The main contract is between you and the seller, who could be either a private individual or a dealer. We have already seen that the legal obligations on a dealer are greater than those imposed on a private individual and your problem is that you may never be able to find out who the seller is. Thus, if the car turns out to be a heap, your chances of obtaining redress are remote and they will be totally dependent on, firstly, whether you can trace the seller and, secondly, even if you do manage that you will still have to prove your case which means finding out whether the car was misrepresented to the auctioneer, who subsequently misrepresented it to you.

Supposing the auctioneer said that the car was a 1300 cc model and that you later find out it had a replacement engine and the replacement is only 1100 cc. If the seller was a private individual you would have to prove that he or she deliberately misrepresented it to the auctioneer who then passed on that information, acting as agent. In order to win your claim, you would have to prove (a) that the seller applied a false description and (b) that he or she knew it to be false.

The seller may tell you that it was not described as 1300 cc and that the auctioneer was not acting on instructions when selling it as such. The only way that you could prove that the seller was lying would be if the auctioneer was prepared to give you a copy of the 'notice of entry', a document giving basic information which must be completed by the seller before the auction, and there is no reason why they should, even if doing so would clear them of any blame. The auctioneer knows that you could not take direct action against them in any event.

If the auctioneer has provided you with a copy of the notice of entry and it shows that the seller wrote on the notice that it was 1300 cc, all the seller has to say in defence is that the car was bought as 1300 cc and that the previous owner must have replaced the engine.

You can see that buying at an auction is a pretty risky business particularly if you are not very knowledgeable, but if you are a gambler and you are aware of the risks then go ahead but remember that cars are generally sold as seen and are not necessarily even sold as being roadworthy. If you drive a car away from an auction and the vehicle is unroadworthy you will be committing an offence yourself.

If you have made up your mind that you are going to buy from an auction, go only to a reputable one, held regularly at the same place and not the sort which is held on a piece of waste land as a one off. Read carefully the conditions posted up on a wall somewhere, or ask the auctioneer for a copy.

Vehicle inspections

25 checks to make yourself

It is your duty to examine carefully a car you are intending to buy. A thorough visual inspection will give you a very good idea of the general state of the car, and it is worth remembering that if the bodywork and the interior have been neglected then it is likely that other things have been neglected too. If later you complain about faults which you ought reasonably to have seen if you had bothered to examine the car, you may lose your rights.

If the seller (whether a dealer or a private individual) tries to discourage you or hurry you, think again. Many people allow themselves to be intimidated by the seller and so fail to make even the most basic checks. A reasonable person will understand that you are spending a lot of money and that you have every right to safeguard your investment. If not, take your business elsewhere.

Do not be hurried by bad weather or failing light. You cannot possibly carry out a thorough examination if it is raining, if the light is failing, or under street lights, so choose a time when conditions are good. If this is not convenient for the seller, then be suspicious. Leave yourself plenty of time and deal with your inspection in two stages. The first stage is all of the items which you can check whilst the car is stationary and the second stage is a road test.

Stationary checks

WITHOUT THE ENGINE RUNNING
1 *Rust and bodywork* Once body rot has gone past a certain point most modern cars are good for nothing but the scrapheap. The problem of rust is becoming increasingly acute for two reasons: the salt now widely used to clear icy roads speeds up the rate of corrosion; and most modern cars have what is called integral or

unitary construction. This means that the body and underframe together provide strength and rigidity (instead of just the frame in a chassis-built car) so that if the body is badly rusted the whole structure is weakened. You may find a little rust, but be very wary if you find a lot especially if it is in the form of pimples and blisters. If possible get the car put on to a lift and look carefully underneath for corrosion at points where there are joins. If there is extensive rot at these points reject the car. Other places to look are the jacking points and the inside of the wings. Do not be afraid to poke gently with a penknife or a small screwdriver – if it goes through, reject the car.

If there is under-body sealing look at it carefully for loose patches. Sealing which is in bad condition acts as a moisture trap and is worse than no sealing at all.

Take a magnet with you and run it around the bodywork to find out whether it has been repaired with body filler. If there are large areas where the magnet does not adhere, the car could either have been badly crash-damaged or suffering from extensive corrosion.

2 *Tyres and wheels* Check that the depth of tread is *at least* the legal minimum (1 mm over the whole width of the tyre) and look for splits on walls both inner and outer, damage to rims and uneven wear indicating misalignment. Make sure all tyres are the same type (ie, radials or crossply) and do not forget the spare.

3 *Wheels* You need to get the car jacked up to check the wheels properly. Stoop down at the side of the car facing the front wheel. Grasp it at the top with both hands and shake it to and from you vigorously. A lot of free play or clunking sounds are signs of loose or worn wheel bearings, worn suspension joints, or worn steering joints.

4 *Suspension* Lower the car back to the road and bounce it on all four corners. When you release it, the car should settle at once at an equilibrium position. If it continues bouncing of its own accord, you can reckon on having to fit new dampers (shock absorbers).

5 *Oil and water leaks* Look under the car for oil and water leaks. A few spots of oil are not sinister but a lot are. And a leaking radiator usually means a new radiator – not a cheap item. But if the leak is from a perished water hose, replacement is a fairly simple matter.

6 *Radiator* Check for obvious signs of repair to the radiator (plastic padding or fibreglass applied to the core or tank areas). Make sure that the radiator is securely mounted. If it is not, check that the hoses have not been weakened through vibration. Check if the hoses are perished or leaking at the joints.

7 *The interior* Check that all the doors open and shut properly, that keys fit and that they lock. Make sure the doors stay open on the hold-open spring if there is one. Pull back the trim from the door edging to see whether there has been a respray. Lift up the carpets and look for rust. Even a few freckles can mean that water seeps in – or soon will. Check for a leaking boot lid, water in the boot can rust through the rear floor. Look at the wear on carpets, seats, upholstery and pedals (the rubbers may have been renewed). Make sure that all windows open and close properly, as well as the bonnet and boot.

8 *Electrics* Now check the horn, windscreen wipers and washers, lights and indicators.

9 *The engine* Examine the engine compartment for any sign of accident repair – new paint or metal, signs of welding, new suspension, buckling or poor alignment. It should be generally clean under the bonnet and not too oily but if it looks *very* clean the car may have been fitted with a reconditioned engine, been cleaned up for the sale, or been given a coat of engine paint. You can tell if the engine has been replaced by checking the engine number against the log book.

10 *Milometer* Now look at the milometer. Does the reading seem a reasonable one, bearing in mind what you have seen of the inside of the car and underneath?

WITH THE ENGINE RUNNING
Now you are ready to switch on the engine. Leave it ticking over because dodgy dealers sometimes put heavy-grade oil in the sump and gearbox to muffle a noisy engine. Wait until the engine is well warmed up before listening for noises.

11 Using a cloth, take off the radiator cap gently. If there is an oil slick or rising bubbles, you can expect trouble – at best a blown gasket, at worst a cracked block or cylinder head.

12 Now look at the dipstick. Do not worry if the oil is dirty, but drops of water or greyish foam could indicate a cracked block.

13 Take off the oil filler cap and watch for fumes or smoke. Either could mean extensive wear and might mean a replacement engine.

14 After the engine has been ticking over for about five minutes or so, rev it up. A worn engine will belch smoke. Blue smoke is the danger signal for costly repairs while black smoke may simply be the result of a carburettor fault, a sticking choke mechanism or over-rich mixture adjustment. Usually these can easily be put right.

15 Have a look at the exhaust pipe to see if there is any sign of white deposits. This could indicate that the fuel/air mixture is extremely weak and could mean valve failure.

16 Now have a look at the battery. Make sure it is fixed correctly and that the terminals are not excessively corroded. Switch off the engine but leave all the lights on for a few minutes and then make sure that the car starts up again without any trouble.

Road test

You are now ready to try the car out on the road – not just once around the block. The test run should include a steep hill, some rough bumpy road and a derestricted stretch where you can go over 50 mph. Make sure *you* drive the car and not the seller who will be able to hold the gear lever in place to stop it jumping out, juggle with a dicey clutch, and so on).

Obviously you must have adequate insurance cover to test drive the car but do not be put off by a dealer who says you cannot drive the car yourself because it is on trade plates. In fact you can drive a car on trade plates, although it is just possible that the dealer does not know this.

Now strap yourself in, and while you are there check to make sure that the seat belts are all functioning properly and that none of them are excessively frayed. The car could fail an MOT test for this.

17 *Engine noises* While driving at about 40 mph in top gear listen carefully for a whine from the final drive (in the back axle in most cars, in the front where there is front-wheel drive). If there is a whine, get it checked. Now drive at about 30 mph in an intermediate gear to detect another transmission fault – backlash; when you

sharply depress and release the accelerator several times, a 'clonk' from the drive axle indicates backlash.

18 *Drive shafts* Check front wheel drive-shafts by driving slowly on full lock and listening for unusual noises.

19 *Big ends* Now test for 'big-end knock'. Accelerate up to high revs in any gear, then take your foot off the accelerator without braking or declutching. If there is a dull irregular knocking, the big end needs replacing. This is an expensive repair. Listen for other unhealthy noises such as misfires, timing irregularity, tappet rattle and piston slap. A short drive over a bumpy stretch of road will show up rattles and squeaks that need attention, as well as jerky or uncertain steering, looseness of the whole front end, and lack of damper restraint (which results in an unduly bouncy ride).

20 *The clutch* Stop the car facing uphill and put on the handbrake, leaving the car in gear. Letting out the clutch slowly should stall the car instantly. If the engine fades gradually, the clutch needs replacing. Watch if the clutch snatches when you are driving away. (Obviously this does not apply to automatics.)

21 *Brakes* Test the brakes – if you have to put your foot down a long way, they will need immediate attention. The same applies if the car pulls to one side when you brake or if there is a grinding noise. If they squeak, check the brake linings; they could be worn down to the rivets and be damaging the brake drum.

22 *Steering* At 30 mph on a straight road without camber, relax your hold on the steering wheel. Any tendency to flutter, vibrate or 'steer off' could mean costly repairs. 'Clonking' and resistance to smooth turning of the wheel means a worn steering box or worn arm joints. Excessive squealing from the front tyres during normal cornering may result from hidden steering and suspension faults.

23 *Wheel bearing* When you are travelling at about 30 mph, slip into neutral and listen. A low-pitched growl means worn wheel bearings. Swing the car from side to side, if this interrupts the noise, a fault exists.

24 *Gears and mountings* During the drive watch for any tendency of the gear lever to jump out when you take your foot off the accelerator. Also listen for clonking and excessive movement when changing gear.

25 *Alignment* Now park the car in a straight quiet road and stand or kneel behind the centre of the car whilst someone drives it slowly away from you. The car that travels a little 'crabwise', with front and rear wheels not in line, has probably been damaged in an accident and should be rejected. You may also detect bent or wobbly wheels, but this is less serious since they can be replaced. Make sure that any wheel wobble is not due to a damaged axle.

Finally, make sure that all extras like tools, radio, etc are included in the price.

If you have been thorough and found nothing which caused you undue concern, you may be ready to do business. It is still worthwhile arranging for an independent engineer to carry out an inspection and provide you with a written report. All of these checks are things which need to be properly interpreted and if you know absolutely nothing about cars at all do not rely on your own judgement. It may be that what you found out will make you want to forget the whole thing and look for a better bargain. Do not persuade yourself, because you love the colour or like the seller, that it will be alright, because it won't. If you have any doubts at all save yourself money and a lot of aggravation by finding yourself another car.

Independent check

If you are not an expert, you should still get the car properly inspected by an independent engineer. You will have to pay for this but it could save you a lot of expense and worry in the future. It can be expensive to have several cars examined. This is why it is important to do your homework before having the car inspected.

If the seller will not wait for you to arrange an inspection, go somewhere else – he probably knows that the car will not do well under expert examination

He may agree to wait if you leave a deposit and if you think this is a good idea then make absolutely certain that you will get your money back if the car fails its inspection. You should get a receipt for the deposit and make sure that written on it are the words 'subject to a satisfactory inspection'.

Assuming that the inspection went well and you are ready to take delivery of your purchase, there are still a few points to watch. First, play safe by checking that the tyres and accessories are all the same as when you made the deal. Next make sure that you have all of the correct documentation. You will need:

- vehicle registration document (log book). The bottom part of the form (regarding change of keeper) will have to be completed and sent to DVLC.

- a receipt. Make sure you get one even if you buy from a private seller. It does not have to be formal just so long as it states the date of sale, the price, details of the car, your name, the seller's name and address, and it should be signed by the seller.

- current MOT certificate (where applicable). Remember it is an offence to drive a car without a valid MOT certificate if the car is more than three years old.

- current road tax – before taking the car on the road.

- current insurance – before you drive the car away.

If you take the car away without the current road tax and current insurance you will be guilty of a criminal offence.

Professional check

A house in need of repair will not kill you, but an unsound car can. The odd thing is that whilst many consumers do not seem to begrudge the money they may have to lay out on abortive house surveys, they are just not prepared to spend a sum which is considerably less on having a car inspected by an expert.

In view of the fact that the average motorist knows very little about what goes on under the bonnet, it should be obvious that it makes good sense to have a thorough inspection carried out by an independent expert before buying a used car. Most complaints arise because a professional inspection was not carried out and because the consumer had not even bothered to give the car the most fundamental of checks before purchase. Often, they had not even taken the car for a test drive.

Obviously, it would be foolish to keep paying for inspections on duff cars, so before arranging for a specialist to have a look at a car carry out the checks detailed on pages 65–70, all of which can be done by a non-expert. Once you have handed over your money to a seller and taken the car away, getting your money back afterwards is a lot harder than waving goodbye to an inspection fee.

Employing independent engineers can be expensive, but the AA or RAC will inspect vehicles comparatively cheaply, although the service is only available to members.

Automobile Association

GENERAL INSPECTIONS
The AA will carry out a general pre-purchase inspection. They would need six to eight working days' notice, and during the summer months this period may be longer. These are complete inspections of the car to assess its overall condition, and are often refered to as 'vet for purchase' which describes the main reason why members ask for them.

Fees vary, depending upon the type of car. The AA will advise on current fees over the telephone.

SPECIFIC INSPECTIONS
These are inspections for specific purposes, such as ensuring that repairs have been properly carried out or assessing the quality of components. The AA should be advised if this is the type of inspection required as the fee is different.

RE-CHECKS
If, after inspection, repairs have been carried out and the consumer wants the work checked, the AA will do this for 50 per cent of the original inspection fee.

ROAD TESTS
Arrangements can be made to road-test members' cars at certain service centres, by appointment. The tests will take about half an hour.

VALUATIONS
The AA will examine vehicles which have been involved in an accident. If, for instance, an insurance company has offered a 'write-

off' settlement which you feel is inadequate, you can take the car to a service centre for evaluation. If the car cannot be driven and an engineer has to see it elsewhere, it will be more expensive. The service is by appointment only. In some cases, the AA will examine vehicles, after an accident, to establish the cause of failure.

COMPONENTS
Arrangements can be made to check small components at certain service centres, by appointment. If it is necessary to examine large components, such as a gearbox, the fee would be the same as a normal inspection fee.

COURT APPEARANCES
AA engineers will give evidence in court if you need to enter into litigation as a result of the engineer's inspection. There is a fee for court appearances but if the hearing is over by midday, it would be reduced by half. If a court appearance is going to be necessary, you should write to the AA giving plenty of notice of the date of the hearing so that the engineer can be available. If the report was carried out some time ago, the engineer should be sent a copy of his report prior to the hearing. The AA does not keep copies of reports which they have carried out for more than four to six months, unless they are advised when the inspection is undertaken that the consumer intends pursuing the matter through the courts.

Royal Automobile Club

The RAC make it clear they will give no advice at all if the consumer is not a member at the time of the purchase of the vehicle.

GENERAL INSPECTIONS
The RAC can carry out an inspection within a week. In the summer, as with the AA, it will probably take longer. If the situation is urgent, some allowances may be made.

The RAC do not like carrying out examinations where they do not have the facility of a pit or a hoist in order to examine the underneath of the car. If an inspection is carried out at a consumer's home and a jack is used to gain access to the underneath, the consumer will be asked to sign an exclusion note to the effect that the engineer accepts no responsibility for the fact that his inspection was limited.

SPECIFIC INSPECTIONS

The RAC will also carry out component examinations provided the car has already been dismantled, but the fee is the same. If you wish to have a small part examined, an oral report can be given for a reduced fee provided the part is taken to an RAC depot. (The value of an oral report is of course questionable.) If the part examined is found to be faulty, a written report can be provided.

ROAD TESTS

The RAC will also carry out road tests provided the car is taken to an RAC depot. The road test will be to examine things like engine or gearbox noises and an oral report, which is cheaper, can be given.

COURT APPEARANCES

The RAC will not, under any circumstances, allow their reports to be used in court. Neither will their engineers give evidence. If a consumer intends pursuing a case to court they should advise the RAC before the inspection is carried out and they will be referred to an independent outside engineer who would be prepared to give evidence. His inspection fee would be roughly the same as the RAC's but any court attendances may be very expensive.

Other engineers

If you are not a member of the AA or RAC and wish to have a potential purchase independently inspected you can find details of other independent engineers in the Yellow Pages or your local telephone directory under 'engineers – motor'.

You should remember that no engineer will be prepared to road test a vehicle which is clearly dangerous.

Finance

Making the decision to take on financial commitments is not as simple as saying 'I can't afford £5,000 for the car so I'll buy it on credit'. If you are going to take on financial commitments you need to be absolutely sure that you are going to be able to afford it, and probably for several years.

There are several types of credit available for buying vehicles. The first step is to make sure that you are getting the best deal. Buying credit should be like buying anything else and you need to shop around to make sure that you are not paying more than you need to.

Annual percentage rate

It has now become law for suppliers of credit to quote the annual percentage rate (APR). It must be shown on any advertisements and you are entitled to be given a written quotation if you ask for it.

You need a common yardstick in order to be able to measure the true cost of the deal, and once you know the APR you can compare the cost of one deal with another by using the APR as a guide. It is worked out in a standard way set down by law and it must include all of the interest as well as other charges made for providing credit. These charges are added together and take into consideration not just the total cost but how and when you have to repay it, so the lower the APR the better the deal.

Even though the terms of any finance agreement may vary greatly, the APR can be applied to all types of credit including bank loans, hire purchase and loans from money lenders. Although the APR is expressed as a percentage it should not be confused with interest rates. For example 'APR 33 per cent' does not necessarily mean you will be paying a flat rate of 33 per cent or £33 on every £100 over 12 months.

Although comparing APRs is the best way to check that you are getting the *cheapest* deal available, there are other things you need to consider to make sure that it is the best deal for you. For example, the APR on one deal may be cheaper but the monthly repayments may be quite high because the loan is over a relatively short period. If you cannot afford high monthly payments then continue looking around for a deal which will suit you better.

What to look for

Once you have decided to buy your car on credit there are several questions you need to ask yourself:

- What is the cash price of the goods?
- How much is the deposit (if any)?
- How much will I need to borrow?
- Have I examined the different types of credit available?
- Have I checked the APR?
- What is the amount and frequency of the payments?
- How long will it take to pay back?
- What will be the total amount payable?

Interest-free credit

Sometimes you may find the offer of interest-free credit. Obviously if it is available it has got to be your best deal but when you look at the contract do make absolutely certain that all of the repayments you will be making add up to no more than the cash price. You may find that you are going to be paying more for 'interest-free credit' because other charges are added on to cover administration. So compare the cash price with the total amount you will be paying on the agreement. You should also check time limits on interest-free credit – for example, the contract may specify that the agreement must be cleared in six months. If it is not, interest will start to accrue and with these kinds of agreements the interest is usually quite high.

Generally, interest-free credit agreements are for shorter periods of time so the amount you have to pay each month could be much more than you can afford.

Arranging the credit

There are two ways that this can be done. Either the dealer will arrange the credit for you or you may choose to obtain the credit yourself.

A dealer must be licensed by the Office of Fair Trading as a credit broker to arrange credit. Failure to hold a licence, or any incorrect details on the licence will constitute a criminal offence. More particularly, any contract which you enter into with the dealer will be unenforceable. This is not the same as voidable. A voidable contract means that both parties must be put back in the position that they were in before the contract was made. If a contract is unenforceable it means that you can simply say 'I am keeping this car and I am not paying you a penny'. The dealer would be unable to take any legal action against you because the contract is not legal.

There are some very important advantages in having the finance arranged by a supplying dealer. Apart from the fact that he will sort out the documents for you because he will already have sources of credit which he can use and therefore get you a cheaper deal, there is a further advantage which you may not be aware of. This is provided by section 75 of the Consumer Credit Act 1974 which says that a finance company has to accept equal liability with the supplier of the goods if the supplier arranged the credit for you. The agreement which you enter into must be what is defined in the Act as a 'debtor–creditor–supplier' agreement as opposed to a 'debtor–creditor' agreement which is arranged by the consumer, and the following diagrams will explain the difference.

diagram 1–debtor–creditor–supplier contract

credit arranged by dealer

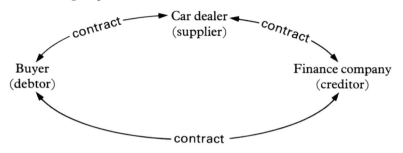

diagram 2–debtor–creditor contract

credit arranged by consumer

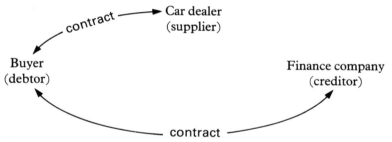

As you can see in diagram 1 there is a connection between the car dealer and the finance company whereas in the second diagram there is no connection between them. The contract exists between the car dealer and the buyer and between the finance company and the buyer but no contract exists between the car dealer and the finance company. This means that the finance company cannot be expected to take responsibility for anything which the car dealer does.

If you arrange the credit yourself, for example by obtaining a loan from your bank manager or dealing with a finance company with whom you have done business in the past, you may be able to get a slightly better deal because the sources of credit available to you may be wider. It has to be remembered that if you are buying privately, there will be no possibility of the credit being arranged for you as part of the deal and therefore you will have to arrange this yourself.

Types of interest

The amount of interest you have to pay is important, but equally important is the way that interest is calculated because this could make a very big difference to the amount of money that you pay in the end. There are fundamentally two types of interest – fixed and what is known as 'revolving' interest.

Fixed interest

This kind of agreement is becoming less common these days but there are still a few around. The agreement will show the cash price of the goods, any deposit which may have been paid, any other 'extras', the total amount of the interest and the total credit price. Here is an example:

Credit agreement (fixed interest)

	£
cash price	2,500.00
'extras' (radio and aerial)	85.00
total cash price	2,585.00
less deposit	500.00
balance to be financed	2,085.00
interest	458.70
total payable	2,543.70
total agreement price	3,043.70

Payable by one instalment of £106.16 on 21 July 1987 and 23 instalments of £105.98 payable on the same date each month thereafter.

The total amount of £3,043.70 will be the full amount you have to pay for the car, regardless of anything which may occur later – helpful if you get into financial difficulty and need to defer your payments.

The agreement will show the dates upon which the payments must be made, and naturally since this forms part of the contract you must adhere to all of the terms of that contract. However, if you should get into difficulty making your repayments or if one of the repayments is a bit late one month, this will not affect the overall price that you pay. The agreement is fixed. The finance company obviously will not be very happy if you do not stick to the terms of the agreement but you will not be financially penalised if you have to reduce the amount of the monthly payments and thereby extend the period over which you pay for the car.

'Revolving' interest

This kind of interest is calculated usually on a monthly basis (in some cases it may be calculated weekly or even daily!). The details on the finance agreement must still be the same, ie they must show the cash price, deposit, total amount payable, etc, but because the interest is calculated differently, you may pay a much greater amount in the end.

In this case the agreement will look the same because, legally, you are entitled to be shown the extent of your commitment on the document you are expected to sign. *But* the important thing to note is that interest is not fixed and added on at the beginning but accumulates on a regular basis and is calculated as a percentage of the amount outstanding. Usually the interest will be calculated monthly on the same date that your payment is due so that if your payment is a few days late, interest will accrue. If you pay £100 one month, instead of the correct payment of £105.98 interest will accrue on the whole balance, not just the £5.98.

One possible advantage of this kind of agreement is that if you pay more each month than you are supposed to, you would incur less interest. Therefore, paying off the agreement sooner could save you money, although technically you would still be in breach of the agreement and the finance company could claim damages because they would not be getting the total amount agreed in the contract.

Credit cards and bank overdrafts for example calculate their interest this way and it means that if the interest is calculated on a monthly basis it will be worked out on the amount currently outstanding at that time. Thus if you do not adhere precisely to the terms of the contract (if your payment is a few days late or you make a payment which is slightly less than it should be) you will incur additional interest charges calculated on the outstanding balance. This means that although you make your payments monthly, you may still find that you pay considerably more than the amount shown on your original agreement.

If you have an agreement which is calculated this way you must make absolutely certain that the monthly payments are exactly the right amount and that they are paid before or on precisely the date specified (that means that they must be in the finance company's account on that day). If your payments are made by standing order make sure that the standing order goes out of your account in plenty of time to ensure that the finance company receives it on or before the date specified on your agreement – standing orders can be paid several days before or after the date that you have requested them.

If you get into difficulty with this kind of finance agreement and arrange with the finance company to reduce your monthly payments, thus extending the life of the agreement, it will cost you a lot more money.

Hire purchase

Hire purchase (HP) works like this: A wishes to buy a car from B who is a car dealer. B arranges credit with C who is a finance company. Technically, B sells the car to C who then hires it to A. The car therefore belongs to the finance company until the final payment when it becomes the property of A.

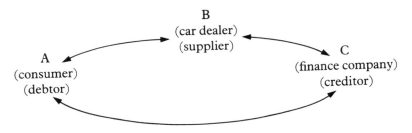

A debtor – creditor – supplier contract

Because the car does not belong to you until you have made your final payment, you may not dispose of it without the permission of the owner. To do so would be a criminal offence (theft).

Insurance

There are a number of other conditions which will always apply when you buy a car on hire purchase and you must be wary of them. For example, the hire purchase agreement will contain a condition that you must insure the car fully comprehensively not just third party. The reason for this is that if anything happens to the car, the finance company will get its money. If you fail to insure the car in this way you will be in breach of contract and the finance company will be entitled to claim damages from you.

When taking out insurance it is important to remember that on the proposal form there will be a question regarding ownership of the vehicle. If you have a hire purchase agreement you do not own the vehicle and you must advise the insurance company that whilst you are the registered keeper of the vehicle you are not the owner. Failure to do so could be considered 'non disclosure of a material fact' and would be grounds for an insurance company refusing to meet any claim (see page 148).

Legal ownership

The finance company is the legal owner. If there are any changes to the car, for example, if you decide to spray it a different colour, if you are involved in any kind of accident, or if you make any structural alterations, these must all be notified to the finance company. You may also find a clause in the contract which stipulates that you may not take the car out of the country without the prior consent of the legal owners. It is unlikely that the finance company would refuse to let you do so, but they must be advised.

Selling the car

If you wish to sell the car before you have finished paying for it, you must obtain the permission of the legal owners in writing and they will quote you a settlement figure which you must pay immediately. If you do not clear the outstanding amount on the finance agreement, the person who buys the car from you will not have 'title' to it, ie legal ownership. If you sell the car without obtaining permission from the finance company the buyer would have a claim against you for breach of contract because there is an implied condition in all contracts that the seller has title to the goods. You would also be committing an offence, and if the finance company chose to report the vehicle as stolen, you could be prosecuted and again any buyer would have a damages claim against you.

Repossession

If you get into difficulty with your payments the finance company would be entitled to repossess the car, although once you have paid one-third of the total amount payable it cannot repossess without a court order.

The finance company will initially give you the opportunity of voluntarily surrendering the goods, and if you are experiencing money worries you may consider that this is a good option – sending the car back will, you may think, be the end of your problems. *Not so!*

You have to understand what happens to the car after it has been repossessed. Finance companies are not in the business of selling cars and so their method of disposing of the car is limited. They are likely to want to get rid of it as quickly as possible and the easiest way to do this is by selling it at auction.

You must remember that you have entered into a legally binding contract with the finance company for payment of a certain amount of money and if you allow the car to be repossessed you are in breach of contract. Whenever there is a breach of contract, the injured party is entitled to damages and the damages in this case would be a sum of money equal to any loss which the finance company has suffered as a result of your breach. This could mean any towing or recovery charges involved, depreciation, etc, and these amounts would be added to the total still outstanding on the finance agreement so that if, when they sell the repossessed car, they do not recover the full amount outstanding, they will be looking to you for the balance.

Here is an example: A buys a car from B (the car dealer). B arranges finance with C (the finance company). A has had the car for three months and then becomes unemployed and so is unable to keep up the payments or continue to run the car. C offers to repossess the car and A agrees. The car is removed and sold at auction but it fetches far less than its original value. First of all, A has done quite a lot of mileage in the car and not looked after it particularly well so it has depreciated. Secondly, the car was sold to A at slightly more than its real value in the first place because B had added on their profit. When the car was sold at auction, C was interested only in getting rid of it for a reasonable amount of money. This is known as mitigating their losses. In other words they are not obliged to recover the full amount of money outstanding on the agreement or even the full value of the car. They are only obliged to recover as much as they can as quickly as they can.

Several months later A receives a letter from C claiming the balance still remaining on his finance agreement and since he is in breach of contract, this amount is due and payable immediately.

Legally, if A fails to make the payment, C will take A to court and will win. The following is an example of how much A will be liable for:

	£
car value	2,100.00
car sold by dealer (including his profit)	2,500.00
A paid deposit of	500.00
leaving a balance of	2,000.00
interest on the balance was	480.00
'option to purchase' fee	3.00
making the total payable	2,483.00
A was to pay monthly over three years so the repayments were £68.88 × 35	2,410.80
plus a final payment (including the option to purchase fee) of	72.20
	2,483.00

A had the car for three months before being unable to keep up the payments. Since the first payment does not fall due until the end of

the first month A had made only two payments on the car. So that
the amount paid was as follows:

	£	£
total payable		2,483.00
deposit	500.00	
two payments of £68.88	137.76	637.76
balance outstanding on the agreement		1,845.24

The finance company then sold the car at auction. Remember that it
was worth only £2,100 in the first place. It is now three months older
and has done quite a few more miles. When sold at auction it fetched
£1,600.

	£
amount obtained at auction	1,600.00
amount paid so far by A	637.76
total received by finance company	2,237.76

The finance company had incurred costs. There was the cost of
arranging for the car to be repossessed and there was the commission
which had to be paid when the car was sold at auction. They have
also incurred storage charges between the time the car was
repossessed and the date that the auction was held. These charges
were as follows:

	£
repossession charges	38.00
auction costs	160.00+
storage charges	42.00+
total	240.00

If we deduct the costs incurred by the finance company (£240.00)
from the total they have received (£2,237.76) we are left with a

balance of £1,997.76. You will remember that the original amount of the agreement was £2,483 so now we must deduct the amount the finance company has from that:

	£
original agreement price	2,483.00
amount received by finance company	1,997.76
balance	485.24

A is now going to be expected to pay the finance company the amount of their damages for A's breach of contract. In other words the finance company is not obliged to be out of pocket in any way as a result of A's breach. A is therefore in a position of having already paid £637.76, having no car, and now owing £485.24. In other words, it will have cost A over £1,000 to have had the use of that car for three months.

The figures that we have used in this example are based on a finance agreement which has fixed interest. If the agreement had been one based on revolving credit, the amount of A's final total liability could have been much more than shown in this example.

The message here is perfectly clear – do not be fooled into believing that allowing a vehicle to be repossessed because you cannot afford it is going to mean the end of your liability.

Equal liability

What are the advantages of hire purchase? Before section 75 of the Consumer Credit Act came into effect, the advantages were that since the finance company was the owner of the vehicle, they had a responsibility to the hirer if the vehicle was defective. For example, if you were hiring a television set and it broke down, you would not expect to have to go on paying the hire charges whilst it was out of order. This is known as 'set off', in other words it is possible for the hirer to set off any damages claim that they may have in respect of a defective vehicle against the amount outstanding on the hire purchase agreement on the grounds that the hirer should not be liable for any hiring charges if the item is defective.

This was why hire purchase was a very good bet for a consumer buying a used car and perhaps not such a good bet from the finance company's point of view, although the advantage to them was that in the event of non-payment they could always repossess the goods whereas if the goods did not belong to them their only remedy would be suing for debt.

The situation regarding all credit has now changed because the Consumer Credit Act bestowed responsibilities on suppliers of finance where there is a debtor–creditor–supplier agreement.

Conditional sale agreement

The legal situation under a conditional sale agreement is very similar to that governing a hire purchase agreement. In other words title remains with the supplier of the finance until the final payment. Therefore all of the above applies to a conditional sale agreement.

Leasing

In many ways a leasing agreement is not unlike a hire purchase agreement but the major and important difference is that title will never pass. In other words, the vehicle always remains the property of the lessor or leasing company. Leases are normally with commercial customers rather than individual consumers.

A contract will usually be for a fixed term, say two or three years, and will require fixed regular payments which may be monthly or quarterly depending upon the contract. Leasing agreements are relatively flexible.

At the end of the term of the lease the property still belongs to the lessor although many contracts contain conditions to extend the term of the lease, usually at a reduced rate, or there may be a facility for the lessee (the person leasing the vehicle) to purchase it at a competitive price.

Contract hire

This is a commercial leasing arrangement most commonly used for fleets of cars or other vehicles. In such an arrangement it is most likely that the lessor will contract to provide an agreed number of particular types of vehicles, rather than specific vehicles, over a fixed period of time. In such an agreement the lessor may also have a contract for maintenance and replacement of any vehicles where necessary and may also include things like road tax.

The advantage to a large company of such an arrangement is that their representatives will always be provided with vehicles in good running order during the term of the contract, without having to worry about the additional expense and inconvenience of having to arrange for the maintenance of vehicles and/or their replacement should they be off the road for any reason.

It is unlikely, however, that most consumers will encounter this type of contract.

As with hire purchase and conditional sale agreements, since the car does not belong to you you may not dispose of it or you will be guilty of theft. And, unlike the other agreements, the vehicle will never belong to you therefore you cannot negotiate with the leasing company to sell it. If for any reason you are unable to keep up the payments, the property simply reverts back to the owners and any payments which you have made will be considered a rental charge which is not refundable. You may also, however, find yourself liable for additional expense as a result of your breach of contract. The leasing company is entitled to argue that the contract which you entered into will ensure that at the end of the agreed period they would have received a specific sum of money and should you wish to terminate that agreement sooner than the agreed period they would be entitled to claim a sum of money equal to any loss which they suffer.

Consumer credit agreement

A consumer credit agreement is also arranged by the dealer and therefore is a debtor–creditor–supplier agreement and you will have to make payments by instalments. The important difference is that the goods become your property as soon as you have entered into the contract. This means that you are entitled to sell or dispose of the goods, although obviously you will have to repay the money outstanding on the finance agreement. You may wish to sell the goods and keep all of the money whilst continuing to make monthly repayments to the finance company and this is not illegal since the goods are yours to dispose of as you like. You must, however, keep up your payments otherwise the finance company will simply sue you for debt.

Under no circumstances can the goods be repossessed since they do not belong to the finance company. The conditions regarding insurance of the vehicle are not as rigid as with a hire purchase agreement, although it is always sensible to make sure that a car is insured fully comprehensively where there is a finance agreement. If the car was damaged or demolished by anyone who did not leave their details or was uninsured, you would still be liable to pay the full amount of the finance agreement even though you may not receive a penny on your insurance or from the guilty party.

Personal loans

Personal loans may be arranged for you by your bank but they are also available in the form of a finance agreement arranged by a dealer and therefore they will still be termed a debtor–creditor–supplier agreement. As with a consumer credit agreement, the goods become yours immediately and all of the terms and conditions are more or less the same.

Arranging the finance yourself

All of the types of credit that we have looked at so far are those which are likely to be arranged for you by a dealer and therefore would fall within the terms of section 75 of the Consumer Credit Act – they would be debtor–creditor–supplier agreements. Now let us examine debtor–creditor agreements. These are the types of finance which you may arrange yourself. Remember that if you obtain the credit yourself the supplier of the credit will have no liability under section 75 of the Consumer Credit Act if anything goes wrong with the goods.

Bank loans

If you have a bank account the most common type of loan is an overdraft, but you can also arrange an ordinary loan or a personal loan. You do not need to have a bank account to apply for a personal loan, although the bank may require some sort of security.

OVERDRAFTS

An overdraft can be a good way of borrowing money particularly if your salary is paid into your bank every month. Remember that the interest is calculated on whatever the outstanding balance on your account is. Therefore, whilst the overdraft might become quite high towards the end of the month, it will reduce and may even be cleared when your salary goes in. The overdraft may then begin to creep up again throughout the month but because the amount outstanding fluctuates, the interest will also fluctuate. In the short term, overdrafts can be the cheapest way to borrow.

ORDINARY LOANS

If you need a fairly large amount of money over a reasonably long period of time you may prefer to arrange to have an ordinary loan. This will allow you to borrow money over a set time where the interest rate will vary and could be quite high.

PERSONAL LOANS

The interest on a personal loan is fixed over a set time and you can arrange with your bank for the monthly repayments to be deducted automatically from your current account and paid to your loan account. Do remember to make sure that there is always sufficient money in your current account to meet the loan repayments. The bank will continue to debit your current account and credit your loan account which could mean that your current account will go into overdraft thus incurring further interest charges.

Money lenders

Borrowing from a money lender can be the most expensive way of obtaining money. Money lenders' risks are quite high, and consequently their interest rates are high.

Money lenders normally have no security and therefore if you default on the payments the money lenders' only recourse is to sue you for debt. Also, if they collect payments from their clients at home, their expenses – and the risk of theft – are going to be higher. Money lenders must be licensed. An unlicensed money lender (loan shark) will be committing a criminal offence if he or she arranges credit for you, and you will be entering into an unenforceable agreement. Do beware of the money lenders who ignore their legal obligations. These kinds of loan sharks not only disregard the law regarding the types of agreements that they enter into, but some of them may also disregard the law when it comes to matters of recovery. Rather than using the courts or other legal remedies to recover the debt they may choose to use some of the distasteful, unpleasant and often dangerous methods of getting back their money.

Legally, a money lender may not call on you at home to sell you credit. No one is allowed to visit to discuss credit without a written request from you to do so. If you are offered credit in this way, the money lender will be committing a criminal offence. Do not confuse this, however, with the situation where a salesman may call at your home to sell you goods on credit. This is legal.

Credit unions

A credit union is a money cooperative run by groups of people with a common interest. It is often a very valuable source of loans. The members may, for example, work at the same place or be members of the same church. By saving regularly, members will become eligible for low-cost loans from the credit union. The Credit Union Act states, among other things, that loans must not incur interest of more than 1 per cent per month. This could make a loan from a credit union the cheapest possible way of borrowing money. However, members must commit themselves to regular savings for a certain period of time before they will be eligible for a loan.

There are not too many credit unions around at the moment and so if you would like to find your local one you can contact the Association of Credit Unions Limited or the National Federation of Credit Unions, whose addresses are on page 233.

Things to watch out for

Whatever kind of credit agreement that you enter into, remember the following:

- do not over commit yourself, check the monthly repayments and make sure that you can afford them before you sign anything

- always check the APR to make certain that you are getting the best deal available

- if you are asked to act as a guarantor for someone else's credit, make sure that you understand what that really means. If they do not keep up the payments you are liable for all of the money. If you are not prepared to pay their credit deal for them do not be a guarantor. If you are prepared to act as guarantor make sure that you have copies of all of the documents. You are legally entitled to them.

- watch out for loan sharks; use only reputable finance companies

- if you are in any doubt about any of the terms of the agreement do not sign it; ask for a copy of it and get advice from your local consumer advice centre or local Trading Standards Department

- remember that once you have signed any kind of a contract you are legally bound by its terms and conditions and you have no right in law to change your mind

- do not just listen to what the salesperson tells you, read anything which is written down; check all of the figures on the contract and make sure that everything is written into the contract; check also that there is nothing written on the contract which was not agreed

- always make sure that you receive copies of any documents that you have signed and keep them somewhere safe

- remember that anyone arranging credit for you must have a licence (the exception is a trader who never offers credit of more than £30)

- remember the dates that your payments must be made (this is especially important on revolving interest agreements)

- if you are arranging for the payments to be made by standing order with your bank, ensure that the standing order is paid in plenty of time for the money to be received by the finance company

- make sure you keep copies of any correspondence, including any letters that you send

- if anything goes wrong with the vehicle and you have a debtor–creditor–supplier agreement always remember to notify the finance company as well as the supplying dealer immediately; do so in writing and keep a copy, no matter how minor the fault

- if you lose your agreement form you are entitled to a copy; write to the finance company and request a new copy

- you are also entitled to a statement if you need to check your repayments; you can obtain one by writing to the finance company.

Refusal of credit

If you go to a dealer to buy a used car and ask him to arrange credit for you, he will complete the necessary documents and there will then be a short delay during which time those documents will be sent to the finance company in order for them to assess your application for credit.

It may be that the finance company do not accept your application. If you are refused credit you are entitled to the return of any money which you have paid (in the form of a deposit or any other charges) and the proposed contract is at an end. The supplying dealer is not entitled to claim any charges from you in respect of that contract.

You may wish to know why you have been refused credit. Legally you are not entitled to a reason. If you think you have been refused on the grounds of race or sex, a criminal offence may have been committed and you should seek advice about this from your local Citizens Advice Bureau.

There are, however, several other reasons why you may be refused credit. For example, a system which is commonly used by finance companies, insurance companies, mail order catalogues and a variety of other organisations is known as 'red lining'. Virtually all of the organisations who practise red lining will deny that they do so but it does exist. In simple terms red lining is the practice of taking a map and drawing a red line around certain housing estates, streets or blocks of flats. The company concerned will then say that they do not do business with anyone living within that area. The practice has evolved because finance companies have found that certain areas, for a variety of reasons, tend to be higher risks than other areas and their records may indicate that people living on certain estates may generally be bad payers. Of course it is possible that you just happen to live in an area which is red lined and if this is so then it is just bad luck. If you have a previously good credit record or you are able to supply a guarantor or some kind of security, the finance company may be prepared to reconsider your application. But short of that, the only way to deal with the situation is to move!

Credit scoring

Currently the most common method of assessing your credit-worthiness is known as 'credit scoring'. This method began in America in the 1940s. It is still relatively new in this country but more and more finance companies and banks are beginning to use it. The advantages of the system are that credit can be obtained relatively quickly and that it is nondiscriminatory. The finance company can see how you score without even knowing your name. The way the system works is that you score points for certain things like whether you own your own home, what you do for a living and so on. If you score above a certain number of points you are considered to be a good risk and below a certain number of points you will not be able to obtain credit.

Credit reference agencies

The other most commonly used practice is the use of credit reference
agencies. The finance company will receive an application from you
and will then contact one of the credit reference agencies for a copy
of your file. The file will contain details of things like county court
judgements and defaulting credit agreements, although in some
cases the file may also show credit arrangements which are currently
running.

On the basis of the information contained on the file the finance
company will then decide whether or not to offer you credit.

Legally, you are not entitled to a reason if you have been refused
credit. You are, however, entitled to see a copy of a credit reference
agency's file on you. The way to obtain a copy of the file is by asking
the trader who has refused your application (within 28 days of the
refusal) for the name and address of the credit reference agency
which he consulted. He is legally obliged to provide this information
if he did consult a credit reference agency. If he did not consult a
credit reference agency then you can proceed no further because he
is not obliged to give you any other reason for the refusal.

Once you have the name and address of the agency, you can write to
them giving them enough information about yourself to make it easy
for them to locate your file – your full name and address and any
previous address if you have not been very long at your present one,
and you must enclose a fee of £1. They are then obliged to send you a
copy of the file.

Included with the copy of the file will be various instructions on
what to do next and you will find these are usually quite clearly set
out. Basically the rights that you have are fairly simple. If the
information on the file is wrong you are entitled to have it corrected.
You must write explaining the situation to the credit reference
agency who will then amend your file and send you a copy of the
amendment. It may be that the information on the file is correct but
that there are mitigating circumstances. For example, the record
may show that you have defaulted on a finance agreement, but the
reason for the default may have been that you were holding a finance
company liable under section 75 of the Consumer Credit Act for
faults with the goods. If this is so you are entitled to write a letter to

the credit reference agency (in not more than 200 words) explaining the mitigating circumstances and the credit reference agency is then obliged to send a copy of your letter with the file every time they receive a request for it.

Early settlement rebates

If you are able to settle an agreement early you are entitled to a rebate of some of the charges. Section 94 of the Consumer Credit Act 1974 gives the right to settle early without being in breach of contract, and it came into effect in May 1985. Section 95 says that you are entitled to receive a rebate of a proportion of the total credit charges.

The rebate must be given whenever an agreement is settled early in full, no matter why. For example, you will receive a rebate if you settle one agreement in order to take out another (these are also known as modifying agreements and there are separate provisions for them); or if you are in default and the creditor demands payment in full (he will have to show the amount of the rebate entitlement when the debt is settled) but you will only be able to claim the rebate when the debt is discharged.

There are legal regulations detailing how rebates are to be calculated. The calculations are extremely complicated so I shall not outline them here but there is a leaflet available from your local Trading Standards Department which explains how the calculations are made. The leaflet is free and it is entitled *Early Settlement Rebates*.

If you do obtain a rebate quotation from a creditor, you can ask your Trading Standards Officer to check the rebate for you to ensure that it is correct.

The law specifies the minimum rebate entitlement and some finance companies may offer a more generous rebate than they are obliged to.

If you wish to exercise your right to settle an agreement early, you must give notice to the finance company in writing. When the finance company receives your written notice, they must first of all determine the settlement date and then calculate any rebate which is due to you. The 'settlement date' is important because it is a term which is used in the regulations and it is the date used for the purpose of calculating any rebate. It may not necessarily be the same date on which you will be required to settle. The finance company will quote you a date by which the settlement must be made. If you do not pay on or before that date, the rebate figure which you have been quoted will be invalidated and it will be necessary for the finance company to quote you a new rebate figure.

The settlement information must be sent to you within 12 working days of your written request and if the finance company fails to supply the information within a month after the 12 days, they will be guilty of a criminal offence. When you receive your settlement statement it must contain the following information:

- a description of the kind of agreement that you have entered into

- the full name and address of the finance company

- your full name and address

- the total amount payable in order to settle the agreement before deducting the rebate

- the amount of the rebate

- a statement to the effect that the rebate has been calculated in accordance with the consumer credit regulations

- a statement explaining where there is no entitlement to a rebate (where applicable)

- the net amount payable

- the settlement date

- a general statement containing information regarding the Consumer Credit Act provisions and where details and advice about it can be obtained.

Once you have all of this information you can settle the agreement by the date shown.

The law and your rights

Warranties and guarantees

Many car dealers offer some kind of warranty or guarantee. There are three main types:

- supplied by the dealer himself (these are usually short-term guarantees, say for three or six months, or up to a certain mileage, and they tend to be supplied free of charge)

- supplied by the manufacturer (these are also often free of charge and usually apply only in the case of new cars)

- independent warranties (these usually have to be paid for and can be quite expensive. They will be for varying periods of time or numbers of miles and they are often referred to as extended warranties).

Remember that you already have rights whenever you buy goods under the terms of the Sale of Goods Act. This law says that if goods that you buy are not as described or prove to be faulty you are entitled to a refund. The law applies whether goods are new or secondhand, so do not be misled by a guarantee or warranty. Your claim is against the seller of the goods and if something goes wrong you do not have to accept less than your legal rights just because you have bought (or may have been given) a warranty.

The background

It may be useful at this stage to look at the history of guarantees. The very first Sale of Goods Act came into effect in 1893. And it was the first time that consumers were given specific protection when they bought goods. The law said (as it still does) that goods must be of merchantable quality, fit for the purpose and as described, bearing in mind age and price, and it goes on to say that if goods you buy are not all of those things you are entitled to reject them and have your money back, provided you do so within a reasonable time.

There was, however, a loophole in that Act making it possible for a consumer to sign away those rights. After the Act had been in effect for a relatively short time, some manufacturers came up with the idea of supplying guarantees. The plan was that the consumer would be offered a manufacturer's guarantee which gave them all sorts of additional rights if that manufacturer's product proved to be defective. The guarantee would be attractively produced offering all sorts of advantages in the event of the product proving unsatisfactory. All of these bonuses would be spelt out in large letters and the consumer would be asked to sign the guarantee and return it direct to the manufacturer as evidence that they had the guarantee.

Most consumers were unaware of the new legislation which gave them legal rights and saw these guarantees as bonuses. Therefore they were only too eager to sign them and send them off to the manufacturer. What most of them failed to notice, however, was that somewhere way down in a corner and in exceptionally small print would be words to the following effect: 'all rights as to fitness for purpose, merchantability and compliance with description, statutory, implied or otherwise are hereby excluded'. Now most consumers, even if they read this, would not have had the slightest idea what it meant. Because they were unaware of the legislation which gave them rights in the first place, they certainly would be even less aware of any bits of paper which sought to remove them. Hence the expression 'read the small print'.

Such guarantees became extraordinarily popular with retailers for two reasons. First, the unwary consumer had been persuaded to sign away all of the rights under the new law which were against the interests of the retailer; and secondly, the retailer was able to use the guarantee as a selling point indicating that if the manufacturer was prepared to offer so many extra benefits, they must be very sure of their product.

By the same token, the manufacturers found that providing such guarantees worked as an equally effective inducement to retailers to buy *their* product in preference to a similar product produced by a different manufacturer who did not provide them with a way out of their legal obligations.

This situation prevailed for a number of years until in 1973 the Supply of Goods (Implied Terms) Act effectively closed the loophole. That law said that consumers could not sign away the rights which the original Sale of Goods Act gave them by simply being unaware of the meaning of an exclusion clause. Later, it actually became illegal to display such an exclusion clause, and even now shops which display notices saying 'no goods exchanged or money refunded' are committing a criminal offence.

Now you may wonder why, if the original point of such guarantees has now been removed, manufacturers' guarantees continue to exist. Basically consumers have come to expect to receive a manufacturer's guarantee whenever they buy new goods. Indeed, many consumers sincerely believe that everything they buy is guaranteed for a year. This of course is not the case. Many of them provide a cheap method of market research. Manufacturers ask a variety of questions such as: 'where did you hear about our product?'; 'how many people in your family?'; 'do you watch Channel 4?'. There is absolutely no obligation on consumers to answer any of these questions and the guarantee cannot be invalidated if they fail to do so, but most consumers willingly fill in such forms giving manufacturers all sorts of information about the purchasers of their products and, in particular, ideas on which types of markets they ought to be aiming at. This kind of market research became a means of obtaining the information at very low cost indeed.

These days, a manufacturer's guarantee is only of any real value if it does give you much more than the law already entitles you to or if there is some good reason why you cannot take up your complaint with the seller of the goods. For example, the seller may have gone bust or closed down, or the goods may not have been bought by you, but were a gift, in which case you could not pursue a claim against the seller as you did not make the contract.

Independent warranties

Towards the end of the seventies, after the law had been tightened up, a new type of guarantee emerged. These were independent guarantee companies which operated in the same way as insurance. A consumer buying a used car, for example, would be offered an independent warranty at relatively low cost (about £30 or £40) which would cover the car for mechanical breakdown in the first year or up to a certain mileage after purchase. There were variations on the same theme but these warranties became extremely popular both with the consumers and more specifically with car dealers.

The less scrupulous members of the used-car fraternity welcomed such warranties with open arms because it relieved them of many of their obligations in respect of defective used cars. Certainly, they would no longer have to worry about expensive items like gearboxes going after about three months because they could now simply refer the irate consumer to the warranty company for these repairs to be done free of charge. However, it also meant that many dealers saw such warranties as an ideal opportunity for them to do no pre-purchase checks, repairs or servicing on cars which they had bought in, before selling them to someone else, on the basis that if anything went wrong it would not be their problem.

Needless to say, many of the warranty companies began to experience serious financial difficulties after a very short time because dealers were simply selling duff cars and totally disregarding their legal obligations. Some of the warranty companies then decided to alter the terms of the warranty so that it did not come into effect until three months after purchase or up to a certain mileage. This safeguard was imposed by the warranty companies on the basis that if a serious mechanical fault occurred within that time, it was the responsibility of the supplying dealer who should have foreseen it. There is, of course, no legal foundation for this assumption but the warranty companies made it a condition in order to protect themselves from some of the rip-offs being perpetrated by the used-car trade.

Even with these safeguards, warranty companies still found themselves inundated with bills for expensive repairs on used cars and as a result many such companies had gone into liquidation by the beginning of the 1980s. A number of lessons, however, had been learned and the independent warranty market still continued to thrive and was very successfully extended to domestic electrical appliances, whilst within the car trade the warranty companies began to impose very rigid conditions which had to be adhered to if the warranty was not to be invalidated.

In many ways, these extended warranties, often very expensive, can now act against the interests of consumers because although some of them provide valuable protection over and above your legal rights, many of them can be of limited value or even worthless. All types of repair or the full cost involved are not always covered. Some cover the cost of parts but not labour and so on. Often there is confusion over who is responsible for the warranty and this can cause delays in settling claims.

Some points to watch

- Most guarantees exclude liability for 'wear and tear' and it can be very difficult to prove that the fault is not due to wear and tear. For example, clutches are usually excluded from the cover provided, even though they are a common cause of failure in used cars. Liability for consequential loss many also be excluded; if your car breaks down halfway through a touring holiday, for example, you may not be able to claim the additional cost of transporting your family home and/or towing the vehicle back – never mind the damages for the loss of your holiday.

- The risk of the warranty company going bust always exists and of course increases the longer the guarantee lasts.

- Is the warranty supplied by the manufacturer, retailer or insurer? This can be a particularly complex issue in the case of extended warranties because most of them, although bought from the trader, are operated by separate commercial companies known as scheme administrators and underwritten by insurers. This uncertainty can cause delays in settling claims.

- Look out for restrictive conditions. For example the product may have to be returned to the seller within a specific period of the fault developing, towing charges and so on may be specifically excluded. The warranty will nearly always contain conditions about regular servicing and may even specify where that servicing must be carried out, eg by a franchised dealer. You may also be required to obtain the dealer's stamp in the warranty booklet to prove such servicing has been undertaken within the time specified.

- Consider the time taken for repairs to be carried out under the terms of the warranty. The warranty company will nearly always want you to supply details of the fault and estimates for the cost of the repairs which must be authorised by them *before* the work can commence. This will involve delays during which time your car is going to be off the road. Usually if you go ahead and authorise repairs yourself and then seek to claim from the warranty company, you will find that the warranty has been invalidated and they will not pay up.

- Do not be influenced by the 'peace of mind' aspect of the guarantee. You may be promised wide protection but if you cannot inspect the details of the guarantee documents until later, you may find that the liability is much more restricted than you were led to believe.

- Consider very carefully the cost of any warranty which you are offered. If you have done your homework and had the vehicle inspected by a qualified engineer before purchase, you may find that you would be better off investing the cost of the warranty and obtaining interest. If a breakdown does occur you will have at least some of the cost towards it and if nothing happens then you have saved your money.

- Finally, always remember that the seller is obliged by law to correct any defects which were there at the time of purchase and he cannot legally exclude liability for such defects. Thus a warranty is only of any value to you if it gives you rights over and above those which are already provided by law.

Legal protection

Whether you buy new or secondhand, and whether or not there is any form of warranty or guarantee, you have legal rights which cannot be taken away from you.

Those rights are set out in the Sale of Goods Act 1979 (which is a consolidating Act, based on the original 1893 Sale of Goods Act and incorporating the provisions of the 1973 Supply of Goods (Implied Terms) Act) which applies to goods sold in the course of a trade or business. In other words, if you buy a new or used car from a dealer the provisions of the Act apply to that transaction.

Whilst this principle works very well in the case of most goods, it is not always so easy to reject a new car. This is because in order to reject and have a full refund, you need to be able to show that the car is simply not fit for use as a car, and in most cases the kind of complaints that people have about new cars are in themselves relatively minor. In other words, they do not make the thing completely useless as a vehicle.

Having said that, it is nevertheless important to safeguard yourself in the event of even a minor fault by rejecting the car immediately, in writing. If you accept even a tiny repair, you will lose your right to reject the vehicle. There is nothing to prevent you accepting repairs but you should always make it clear, in writing, that you are accepting them 'without prejudice' so that should the repairs prove unsatisfactory or should the car break down again with another, more serious fault, you will not have lost your rights.

The Sale of Goods Act does not apply to private sales. It may be helpful to be sure about the meaning of 'in the course of a trade or business' because some dealers have been guilty of advertising cars without making it clear that they are dealers. They do so because they know that a consumer's rights are greatly reduced if the car is sold privately. However, failure to specify that the seller is a dealer is an offence under the Business Advertisements Disclosure Order 1977 which says that for a dealer to advertise vehicles for sale in classified advertisements, they must state that they are in business. And if they fail to do so it is a criminal matter, enforced by local Trading Standards Departments. This order was designed to protect prospective purchasers from dealers posing as private sellers because they may have been misled into believing that they had no rights if something went wrong with the car that they bought.

There has been much controversy in the courts regarding what constitutes a business sale – particularly where cars are concerned. For example, there was a case where a man who was unemployed often had old bangers for sale in the street outside his house. When a consumer claimed redress through the courts because the car she bought turned out to be fit only for scrap, the seller sought to have her case dismissed on the grounds that she was claiming under the provisions of the Sale of Goods Act which did not apply to him because he was not a dealer. He argued that it was a private transaction and she had no claim against him.

The registrar who was hearing the case pointed out that the log book made it clear that the seller was not the registered keeper and asked who it belonged to. The seller replied that he was 'selling it for a friend' so the registrar asked whether the other cars he had for sale were also being sold for friends to which the seller replied that they were. The registrar then wanted to know whether these 'friends' paid him a commission for selling their cars and the seller said that they did not. The registrar, naturally enough, queried why he spent so much of his time doing these 'favours' if he got nothing out of it. The previous owner of the car was contacted and made a statement to the effect that the car had been sold outright to the seller for the sum of £250. The seller subsequently sold it to the claimant, only three weeks later, for £450.

When this statement was produced, the seller's response was 'Ah well, this actual car is not being sold for a friend. *This* one I bought for my own use and then decided not to keep it.' Further enquiries relating to the other cars currently on offer outside his house showed that each car displayed a price on the windscreen which was anything up to 150 per cent profit on the sum paid by the seller to the previous owners.

The registrar held that since he was selling cars for profit at a rate of several cars a month, he could be termed a dealer.

The point is that a seller does not have to operate from a showroom in the high street, or even a tatty lock-up under the railway arches, to fall within the constraints of the Act and the message is – beware of the dealer masquerading as a private individual.

Contract

There are many different sorts of contracts, some of which (eg for land or employment) must be in writing, but for our purposes we only need to know about the simplest rules of contract.

A contract is an agreement between two or more people. It is legally enforceable and is dealt with by civil law, which means that in the event of a breach of contract the only person able to take action is the aggrieved party. An oral contract is just as legally binding as long as it has the following three elements:

- *Offer* The offer must be genuine and it can be made orally, for example on the telephone, by radio or television; in writing, eg by letter or advertisement; or by implication or conduct, eg at an auction.

- *Acceptance* The acceptance must be genuine and unqualified. It must comply exactly with the offer, otherwise it could be considered a counter-offer.

- *Consideration* The definition of consideration is 'some right, interest, profit or benefit accruing to one party, or some forbearance, detriment, loss or responsibility given, suffered or undertaken by the other'. Consideration usually, therefore, means the amount of money being paid, but can be anything upon which there is a value, for example time.

Terms of contracts (clauses)

These are the conditions on which the contract is made. Some terms are not enforceable, but those which were known, or should have been known, by both parties when the contract was made are enforceable.

The law assumes that people read conditions on receipts and written contracts as well as any conditions which may be displayed on notices where the transaction takes place.

Certain contracts may be made void by a court. For example those made by minors, lunatics, inebriates and drug addicts.

Breach of contract

This is when one of the parties breaks any of the terms of the contract.

Breach of condition or warranty

A condition is a fundamental term of the contract, vital to the contract. Warranty is a relatively minor term and not as important as a condition. For example, if you bought a car which was to be delivered on Tuesday, and it was never delivered that would constitute a breach of condition. If it was delivered on Wednesday, instead of Tuesday it would be considered a breach of warranty and you may be entitled to claim damages (an amount of money) for loss of use.

Claims

Any claim that you may have against a trader has to be between those who are party to the contract. In other words, you could not take action directly against a manufacturer because you have no contract with the manufacturer. Your claim is directly against the seller who has complete responsibility for the goods he sells. The seller may have a claim against a manufacturer but that is the seller's problem. Any claim that you may have against a trader for breach of contract is a civil claim. This means that you would have to take action yourself. Such claims are not enforced by the police or Trading Standards Departments or any other enforcement authority. If you were unable to obtain your rights by negotiation, you may be forced to pursue your claim to court. You could employ a solicitor to help you take your claim or you may choose to do it youself (see page 115).

Sale of Goods Act 1979

As we have already said, this law encompasses the original Sale of Goods Act 1893 and the Supply of Goods (Implied Terms) Act 1973 which dealt with some of the loopholes in the original law. It sets out the basic rights between buyers and sellers which exist in contracts for the sale of goods.

For most of us, acts of parliament are complicated and difficult to read. This one is no exception even though most of its provisions, when explained in simple terms, seem like nothing more than common sense. It is necessary to understand the basic provisions of the Act because it is so fundamental to our rights in all cases when we buy goods. Probably the most important sections are section 13 (which deals with sale by description) and section 14 (which deals with implied terms about quality or fitness). In essence, section 13 says that goods which you buy must correspond with any description applied to them, and section 14 says that where a seller sells goods in the course of a business there is an implied condition that the goods are of merchantable quality and fit for the purpose.

Compliance with description is reasonably straightforward but the term 'merchantable quality' has caused difficulty over the years both for consumers and lawyers. Merchantable quality means fit for the purpose for which goods of that kind are normally used, having regard to any description applied to them, price and other relevant factors. For example if you bought a secondhand car you could not expect it to perform as well as a new car. You should reasonably expect some defects. However, the extent of the defects is the issue which has never really been sufficiently clarified.

The implied condition as to fitness is reasonably clear. A motor car needs to be fit only for the purpose of driving along the road. If you required a car for any other purpose, you would not be entitled to assume that the car was suitable unless you had made your specific needs clear to the seller and then relied upon his skill and judgement in deciding whether or not to buy the car. For example, if you had a large family caravan which you wanted to tow and you had decided to buy a little three-wheeled vehicle such as a Reliant, and you bought the car from a dealer without describing its intended use, it would be completely unreasonable for you to ask for your money back if the car turned out to be unsuitable for towing your caravan. However, if when you went to buy the car you made it absolutely clear to the dealer what you wanted it for and the dealer advised you that the car would be suitable, you would be relying upon his or her expertise, and if the car subsequently turned out to be unsuitable, you would have a claim against the dealer.

Merchantable quality is much more difficult. It has to be remembered that this law applies to new and secondhand goods (it also applies to goods which have been reduced, such as in a sale or because they were damaged). *Caveat emptor* means 'buyer beware', and there is an obligation on buyers to examine goods, as far as it is reasonably possible, to ensure that those goods are going to be suitable for the purpose and that the goods are not seriously defective or damaged. In the case of a used car, you would be expected to examine the car carefully for cosmetic faults and any other damage or faults which could easily be seen, and you would also be expected to take the car for a test drive. You would not be expected to strip down the engine and gearbox to make sure that all the parts were in order.

If you have taken all reasonable steps to safeguard your purchase and a fault then manifests itself which you could not reasonably have known was there at the time of the purchase, then you may still have a claim against the seller provided that you can argue that the fault was inherent, ie there at the time of purchase. Now in the case of used cars this can often be quite difficult to prove. You would expect a car with 35,000 miles on the clock to be in need of some repairs which are the result of wear and tear, although if a major breakdown occurs within a very short time after purchase it may be equally reasonable for you to argue that the seller, as an expert, should have known that such a major repair was imminent. On the other hand, there are some problems which can occur with cars as a result of wear and tear which are not foreseeable and which can happen at any time. Your problem if you are seeking to make a claim against the seller is going to be that of proving that the fault was there at the time the car was sold to you and that the seller knew or should have known of its existence.

Trade Descriptions Act 1968

In addition to the civil law rights with regard to descriptions, conferred by the Sale of Goods Act, the Trade Descriptions Act makes it a criminal offence to apply a false description. This means that apart from being able to claim redress, ie a refund or damages, the supplying dealer may be prosecuted if he falsely describes a vehicle. The consequences of a criminal prosecution are a fine and, in certain circumstances, the possibility of a prison sentence. This legislation is enforced by Trading Standards Departments. In order for a Trading Standards Officer to achieve a successsful prosecution, a number of elements must be satisfied. For example:

- the Act makes it an offence to supply or offer to supply goods falsely described

- the supply or offer must be in the course of a trade or business

- the description must be false to a material degree and this must be proved

- it is an offence for a dealer to imply (by displaying a logo or symbol) that he or she is a member of a trade association when that is not the case

- it is an offence to claim work having been carried out when that is not true, for example if a dealer said that an engine had been reconditioned when it had not, this would be grounds for prosecution.

Section 2 of the Act provides an exhaustive list of those things which can be considered a trade description. It includes such matters as quantity and size, method of manufacture, date of manufacture or production, prices, price comparisons, false descriptions, etc.

Remember, though, that the statement must be made in the course of trade or business. Any false descriptions applied in a sale between private individuals would not constitute a criminal offence. That does not necessarily mean, however, that you may not have a claim in a private transaction but it would be necessary to prove misrepresentation (see page 111).

Road Traffic Act 1972

Section 60 of the Road Traffic Act 1972 makes it a criminal offence for anyone to sell an unroadworthy vehicle, unless it is made clear to the buyer that the vehicle is suitable only for parts or for scrap or that it needs major repairs. This is the case whether the vehicle was bought from a dealer or privately. The law is enforced by the local Trading Standards Department or the police. If the seller does not make it clear that the car should not be used on the road in its present condition then an offence will have been committed if the car is found to be unroadworthy.

Unroadworthy means that the car is not fit to be driven on the road. In general the sorts of items which will be examined will be the same items that would be tested during an MOT test. However, the fact that a vehicle has an MOT certificate is no guarantee of its roadworthiness because the MOT certificate may have been granted a long time ago. Although an MOT certificate is valid for a year, an awful lot of things can go wrong with a vehicle during that time. Equally, the fact that a car *does not* have an MOT certificate does not necessarily mean it is unroadworthy. There are a number of reasons why a car may be supplied without an MOT. Naturally the car has to be three years old before it legally requires one but the certificate may have been lost or recently expired.

It is very important to examine any documents that you are given when you buy a car – including the receipt. It is not uncommon for rogue dealers to stamp receipts 'sold for scrap' or 'sold for parts'. Such exclusion clauses may even be printed (in very small print) somewhere on the receipt, and if so, the dealer would have a valid defence to a prosecution under section 60 of the Road Traffic Act. I have come across many such receipts when consumers have complained that a car they have bought is unroadworthy. In most cases the consumer had either not read the receipt or not thought that it was important.

Misrepresentation Act 1967

There are three main categories of misrepresentation – fraudulent, negligent and innocent.

Fraudulent misrepresentation

Fraudulent misrepresentation applies when a false statement is made and the seller clearly knew it not to be true. The remedy for fraudulent misrepresentation would be rescission of the contract (in other words the contract would be voidable) and damages. The damages would be any loss suffered by the buyer, whereas in most cases a damages claim must be for damages which are foreseeable.

For example if you were buying a vehicle and were then going to take it abroad on holiday and your holiday was ruined because of the breakdown of the vehicle, you would be able to claim any expenses that you have incurred even though you had not made it clear to the seller that you were about to take it abroad. In virtually all other cases where damages are claimed, the damages must be foreseeable.

Negligent misrepresentation

This is a bit more difficult to deal with but in essence it means that the seller makes a statement without caring whether it is accurate or not, in other words, will make representations about the vehicle 'recklessly'. Once again, the remedy would be rescission of the contract and damages, but in a case like this the damages would be only those which were foreseeable.

Innocent misrepresentation

As implied, the important issue here is that although a vehicle may have been misrepresented, it was done innocently. If A bought a car, and when buying it was told that various things had been done to it, including that it had been fitted with a new engine, and shortly after purchase decides to sell it again, when selling the car A would tell the present buyer that the car has been fitted with a new engine. Later the buyer finds that this is not true. There is little doubt that the vehicle would have been misrepresented but the seller would be relying upon information supplied by a third party (the first seller) which A had no reason to disbelieve. The remedy for innocent misrepresentation would be either rescission of the contract or damages, but not both.

Rescinding a contract

A few brief words about rescission may be useful here. We have already seen that rescission means that the contract is voidable, in other words it is valid until it is called off. Courts will only grant rescission when it is 'just and equitable' to do so and it means that the innocent party must be put back in the same position that he was

in before the contract was made. Sometimes, of course, this is
not possible, and in such a case the only alternative is damages
(money).

Here is an example of where rescission of a contract would not be
possible: you buy a used car for £1,500 and you part exchange your
own vehicle on which the dealer allows you £500. Thus, you have
paid £1,000 in cash and been given an allowance of £500 for your car.
You later find that the car you bought is defective and you therefore
claim rescission of the contract (this applies in the case of the Sale of
Goods Act, Misrepresentation Act or other breach of contract). The
dealer is prepared to take back the used car and refund your money
but he has already sold the car you part exchanged, therefore it
simply is not possible to put you back in the position you were in
before the contract was made. You would, however, be entitled to
the £1,000 you had paid plus damages equal to the value of your
part-exchanged car, ie £500.

Taking your case to court

Legislation under the Trade Descriptions Act, Consumer Credit
Act, Business Advertisements Disclosure Order and Road Traffic
Act is a criminal matter which is enforced by the local Trading
Standards Department (that is the trading standards department in
the area where the contract took place). The Road Traffic Act is also
enforced by the police.

A brief outline of the difference between criminal and civil law may
be useful at this point. In a nutshell, criminal law seeks to punish
and civil law aims to compensate victims.

The onus is very much on you as buyer to take all reasonable steps to
safeguard yourself against being ripped off. You should examine
vehicles as far as it is reasonably possible to do so, you should ask all
the right questions, you should get things in writing and you should
verify any information that you are given. However, it is still
possible, even when you have been fairly careful, to end up with a
lemon because some unscrupulous car dealers are pretty clever. But
if a seller does commit a criminal offence when he sells you the
vehicle, getting some kind of compensation can still be a problem.

Conviction of a criminal offence may cost a dealer a fine but it will not automatically solve your problem – namely that you have a duff car. It may be quite a long time before the case comes to court and even when it does, magistrates will not award compensation to the buyer as a matter of course. Even when it is applied for, any award which is granted may be far less than the loss which you have sustained. Therefore you will need to take civil action against the seller to claim damages and this could be done whether or not any criminal action were pending. Even if a trader is being prosecuted by the police or the local Trading Standards Department, there is nothing to stop you taking a civil claim against the dealer at the same time.

If no offence has been committed, for example, if the seller is in breach of contract, you would have a claim under the Sale of Goods Act but in civil law no official 'body' will take action for you. It is for the aggrieved party to pursue the claim. You may wish to employ a solicitor in order to help you make a claim against a seller but this can be quite expensive and is not always necessary. It may be relatively simple and straightforward for you to take your case to the county court and you could do this on your own.

County courts

The county courts were established by the County Courts Act 1846 in order to deal with civil matters. There are over 400 county courts; these are divided into groups called circuits, and a judge is appointed to travel the circuit from court to court. The judge is assisted by the registrar of the court who is a solicitor and hears many of the cases himself. Although most cases are heard by the judge or registrar alone, occasionally there may be a jury.

The majority of cases dealt with by county courts are default actions – summonses for nonpayment of a debt. They also deal with possession summonses for nonpayment of rent; all sorts of actions regarding defective goods or services; claims arising out of road accidents; certain matrimonial actions such as custody cases; and so on. The county courts can deal only with actions which arise within their geographical area and for claims not exceeding £5,000.

Since 1973 an arbitration procedure has been available to settle certain types of dispute, and both parties must agree for the case to be heard by arbitration. This applies only to claims for less than £500. The procedure has been made simple and straightforward specifically in order that individuals can pursue claims themselves without needing a lawyer. There is a booklet entitled *Small claims in the county court – how to sue and defend actions without a solicitor*, written by Michael Birks who is himself a county court registrar. The booklet is available free from any local county court.

Making a claim

The first step would be to go to the local county court and collect a request for a summons form. The court staff will help you to complete the form but they are not allowed to give you advice regarding the law or the merits of your case. The person issuing the summons is the plaintiff and the person being sued is the defendant. Once you have completed the form you will be required to pay a fee. The cost of issuing a summons is 10 per cent (10p in the £) of the amount you are claiming with a minimum fee of £7 and a maximum fee of £43. The cost is broken up as follows: £70 – £300 is 10 per cent; £300 – £500 is £37; £500 – £5,000 is £43. The fee has to be paid when handing in the completed summons form and the cost of the fee will be awarded against the defendant if the plaintiff wins.

Summonses are normally served by ordinary mail, although they can be served by a bailiff which will cost an extra £5. In certain special circumstances you may wish to serve the summons yourself in which case you can do so but you will be required to go back to the court within four days and swear an affidavit that you have served it.

The summons will be given a case number (sometimes called a plaint number). It is very important that you keep this number safe because all cases are recorded by numbers and cannot be traced any other way. Once the summons has been served there are several things which the defendant can do:

● submit a defence

● pay the amount claimed into the court

● submit a counterclaim.

Sometimes the defendant will ignore the summons. If this happens judgement is likely to be awarded by default. In other words, it is assumed that if the defendant fails to defend the action that there is no defence and the plaintiff will be awarded judgement.

If the defendant pays the amount claimed into court, then that is the end of the action and naturally there is no need for a hearing.

If the defendant submits a defence or counterclaim then a date will have to be fixed for a hearing. The first hearing – the preliminary consideration (also known as the pre-trial review) – is an opportunity for the registrar to give directions as to how the case should be dealt with: whether there will be any witnesses called, how long it is likely to take, whether there are documents to be exchanged, and so on.

If it is a reasonably straightforward claim, the registrar will do his best to settle it at this first hearing. Otherwise, he will simply give directions and a further hearing will then be required. Each party will be asked to sumbit a list of the documents they intend to produce during the case and these lists must be exchanged so that both parties know in advance what sort of evidence is going to be given. Each party is then entitled to have copies of any documents if they need them.

If a counterclaim has been issued (and a counterclaim may not necessarily bear any relation to the original summons) this will have to be heard as a separate action, although most actions will be heard at the same time.

On the day of the hearing the plaintiff will be required to put his or her side of the story and then the defendant will be given an opportunity to ask any questions. It will then be the turn of the defendant to put his or her side of the story and for the plaintiff to ask questions. The registrar may also ask questions of either side in order to help make his decision. The proceedings will be informal and usually they will be held 'in chambers' (in the registrar's office or smaller courtroom) and it is likely that the only people present will be the parties to the action.

The registrar will make his decision there and then and his decision is final. The only grounds for appealing against a registrar's decision are:

- if he was wrong in law
- if he misconducted a hearing
- if there is new evidence.

If the plaintiff wins, the defendant will be ordered to pay the money into the court within a certain time, probably 14 days. The defendant may not be able to pay all of the money in one go. An arrangement can then be made for so much a month to be paid into the court office and that money will then be sent to the plaintiff. If judgement is awarded by default – either because the defendant ignored the summons or failed to turn up for the hearing, or if the plaintiff wins the case and the defendant fails to pay the money into the court as ordered, it may be necessary for the plaintiff to look for some method of enforcing the judgement.

There is another very useful book, also available free of charge from the county court, entitled *Enforcing money judgements in the county court – how to obtain payment without a solicitor* which details the different methods available. There are several methods of enforcement, but the following two are those most commonly used. A 'warrant of execution' means that the bailiffs can call on the defendant and seize goods to the value of the judgement. An 'attachment of earnings' order, is a means by which the amount of the judgement is deducted regularly from the defendant's salary at source.

If you need further help or advice before issuing proceedings or once the proceedings have been issued you should go to your local consumer advice centre or Citizens Advice Bureau.

 # Servicing

Complaints

A report on car repairs and servicing by the Director General of Fair Trading, published in July 1985, suggests that over 10 per cent of consumers, (some one and a half million people per year) have something to complain about after a visit to a garage. Most complaints are about the garage not completing all of the work required, or not doing the work properly, though a few were about the cost of the work.

Research for the report revealed that most people discussed the matter with the garage. Very few approached a third party, but even so the number of complaints made to advice agencies about car servicing and repairs continued to rise from 10,155 in 1982 to 11,806 in 1984. Many people do not complain to anyone, either because they think they have no rights or because they feel foolish.

In April 1984 the Consumers' Association reported in *Which?* that out of 40 services carried out, only 8 were done reasonably well.

There are various reasons why servicing poses so many problems. Apart from laziness, dishonesty or just plain incompetence, the way that many mechanics are paid influences the quality of the work.

Manufacturers provide service schedules specifying the amount of time to be allowed for each job. A number of garages offer a bonus system to their mechanics whereby the bonus is paid for each job provided that it is completed in considerably less time than the manufacturer allows. Clearly if a mechanic is going to be paid more money for doing a job speedily rather than for a job well done, consumers are in danger of getting a second-rate service and a hurried mechanic is much more likely to make mistakes.
A large proportion of blame, however, must rest with consumers themselves. Most consumers do not give clear instructions when

leaving their car at a garage and many of them do not even ask for an estimate or a quotation.

If you take a car into a garage and say to the mechanic 'there is a noise under the bonnet could you please put it right – I'll be back to collect it at 6 o'clock' you have given them the right to do anything to that car which they consider is necessary and if when you go back at 6 o'clock you find that they have put in a new engine and your bill is several hundred pounds you will be obliged to pay it.

Labour charges can be as high as £20 an hour (depending on where you live) and that does not include VAT. The high cost of repairs coupled with the motor trade's generally bad reputation has encouraged more and more people to do their own servicing. It is estimated that more than four million people carry out their own servicing and repairs, and because of this there has been an increase in the number of garages which will provide facilities for do-it-yourself. This can be invaluable if you do not have off-street parking or a garage at home. These garages usually charge an hourly rate and will also hire out equipment and tools.

Even if you are wary of carrying out fairly complex repairs or undertaking jobs which affect the safety of the vehicle such as replacing the brakes, most people should be able to carry out straightforward servicing such as changing the oil and replacing the plugs themselves.

It is worth investing in a course on car maintenance. You can obtain details of courses run by your local authority from the local authority itself or from your local library. Many of these are available in the evenings and are very cheap.

Redress under the law

It used to be extremely difficult to obtain redress if you were dissatisfied with the service provided by a garage. The terms and conditions of a contract are those which are said or written down at the time when the contract is entered into. The major problem is that people are not specific when arranging for their car to be repaired or serviced.

If it is important to you that your car is back on the road by a certain time and if you are not prepared to pay more than a certain amount for work to be done, then you must make this absolutely clear at the outset and preferably put it in writing. It then becomes a condition of the contract and if the repairs take longer or the price is much higher, the garage will be in breach of contract.

Supply of Goods and Services Act 1982

Given that consumers have for years been very vague about services in general, there was clearly a need for legislation in this area and such legislation came into effect in 1983. The Supply of Goods and Services Act, while not introducing any 'new' rights, tidied up the law on consumers' rights and traders' obligations (the Act, however, does not apply to Scotland).

The Act is in two parts. Part 1 is broadly concerned with goods and Part 2 with services.

Goods

The Act provides that, goods which are supplied – as part of a service, on hire, and in part exchange, must be of merchantable quality, fit for the purpose and as described.

Before this law came into effect it was difficult in certain circumstances to know exactly what your rights were and it was harder for you to get your money back if you had a complaint. For example, if you went to a garage and bought a gasket and fitted it yourself you would be entitled to your money back if the gasket turned out to be faulty, but if you took your car to the garage for a mechanic to fit a gasket (the gasket being obtained as part of a service) the situation was not so clear cut and claiming your money back was a good deal more difficult.

Again, a few years ago, when business was bad, car dealers were offering inducements on certain models of cars, such as a free portable television with a certain model of car, if bought within a certain time. The television would be a major inducement in your decision to buy the car from that dealer at that time but if the

television later proved to be defective then the whole deal would not
have been such a bargain as it appeared. Some of these inducements
still exist, but this sort of contract is now covered by the Supply of
Goods and Services Act.

Services

Part 2 of the Act specifically deals with services and it specifies that
any person providing a service for you must do so – with reasonable
care and skill; within a reasonable time; and for a reasonable charge.

Now the question of what is reasonable would have to be decided by
comparison with the 'normal' price, time and standard for providing
that particular service.

Work should be carried out with reasonable care and skill, and this
applies in all cases. It is a right which cannot now be taken away
from you. As to the length of time taken and the charge, these rights
now apply even when nothing has been said when the contract was
made about time or cost. In the case of car servicing, the
manufacturer or one of the motoring organisations would be able to
tell how long a certain job should take and the cost of the part. Thus
it would be possible to argue that something had not been done
within a reasonable time or that you had been charged too much.
You would have to take account of varying local labour charges and
of course VAT will be added on. You still also need to take
reasonable steps to be clear about exactly what kind of contract you
are entering into.

For example, you may obtain a quotation in advance which is
extortionate but if you agree to an excessively high price, without
question, you may still have to pay it unless you can argue
extenuating circumstances. Such circumstances could exist if your
car breaks down miles away from anywhere and you call a
breakdown service whose mechanic tells you that he can do the
repair immediately but that it is going to be expensive. You may feel
that you have no choice because you cannot get the car home and you
cannot find anybody else at that time or place to do the repair for
you. In a case like this a court would probably agree that the
mechanic was taking advantage of your situation and that you would
only be obliged to pay a reasonable price. However, if you have the

option of shopping around for a good deal and just do not bother to do so you may find it much more difficult to prove your claim after the event.

You should also protect yourself further by insisting, when you agree to leave your car for repair or servicing, that if the mechanic finds any other problems once he starts work on the car that he does not continue with the repairs until he has received your authority to do so, and you should be sure to provide him with a telephone number where he can contact you in a hurry.

If a certain time has been quoted for the repairs and it is important that you have your car back by the date agreed then you must make that clear when you leave it. You must make 'time of the essence' and preferably do this in writing. You cannot claim damages for loss of use of the car unless you advised the mechanic in advance that it was particularly important.

If there is something wrong with your car and you do not know what the fault is, the best way to ensure that you are getting a good deal is to take it to three different garages and ask each one of them to give you an idea of the problem, how much it is likely to cost and how long it will take. If two garages come up with the same fault, the chances are that that is what is wrong. Then choose the cheapest or quickest estimate depending on which is most important to you. Then make sure that you have confirmed the agreement in writing.

After repairs have been done to your car you should ask for full details of what repairs have been carried out and a breakdown of the cost of each item should be written on the receipt before you hand over your money. A very common problem is arranging for repairs to be done and shortly afterwards the car breaks down again. The unhappy consumer returns to the garage explaining that all the symptoms are the same and that the garage clearly cannot have done the repairs properly in the first place. The mechanic is very likely to say 'It's a different fault. We'll repair it but you'll have to pay.' If you did not obtain a detailed, itemised receipt you will not be able to argue.

If you have an itemised receipt and the car develops what appears to be the same fault, obviously your first step is to return the car. If the mechanic then tells you that the fault is something different, before you take his word for it get someone else to have a look over the car for you to make sure that what he is telling you is correct. If another mechanic inspects the car and advises you that parts which have been fitted are defective or that work has not been carried out properly try to get him to put that in writing and then go back to the first mechanic and ask him to carry out remedial work at no charge.

You may have difficulty in obtaining something in writing from another garage and in a case like this you may have to prove your claim by getting an independent report done by one of the motoring organisations or an independent engineer. This is going to cost you money. You must therefore make it absolutely clear to the mechanic that if you have an independent inspection done and it confirms your contention that repairs have not been carried out correctly, you will expect to be reimbursed the cost of the report (see draft letter).

It is important to give the garage an opportunity to respond to your letter (you could be arranging a provisional date for the inspection in the meantime), as, if the garage then offered to carry out remedial work free of charge and you had already had the report done, you wouldn't be able to claim the cost. Equally, if such a case eventually went to court and you could not prove that you had forewarned the garage of your intention, you would not be awarded these costs.

If you do not receive a response to this letter, go ahead with the inspection and then write again.

If your car is taken for repair and you have taken no steps to safeguard your interests, you may find yourself in the position of having a bill for work which you did not ask for. If you refuse to pay the bill the mechanic will simply refuse to release your car, and if you do pay, you will find it very difficult to claim back some of that money later unless you make it absolutely clear that you did not agree with the price charged for the work done.

Catch 22 – either you pay the money or you don't get your car back. So what's the answer?

Well, if you can afford to be without the car you could leave it there and then make a claim against the garage. The problem with this course of action is that if they are real cowboys they may undertake other 'remedial work' on the car while it is in their possession. This, of course, could prejudice your claim. Worse than that, they may

Your address

Date

The name and
address of
the Garage

Dear Sir

Re: <u>Make and Model of Car, Registration No. xxxx</u>

On x date I took the above car to you for repair.

I collected the car on x date and paid £x (your
invoice No. x).

The following day, I noticed that the car had
the same faults as when I took it to you for repair.

I returned the car to you on x date and you advised
me that it was a different fault and that if I
wanted it repaired, I would have to pay again.

I do not believe that you have carried out the
repairs properly and I therefore intend to have
the car independently inspected. If the inspection
confirms my belief then I shall expect you to put
the car right at no charge (after which I shall have
it re-inspected), and to reimburse me the cost of
the report.

If I do not hear from you within seven days I shall
proceed as outlined above.

Yours faithfully

Draft letter of complaint about inadequate repairs

refuse to accept responsibility for the car and move it into the street or if they are prepared to keep it in their garage, they may tell you that since the work has been done, if you are not prepared to pay their bill and take it away you will incur a daily storage charge.

Your best course of action is to remove your car, and the way to do it without prejudicing any claim you may have against the garage is to state that you are paying 'under protest'. You should put this in writing either on the mechanic's own copy of the receipt or on a piece of paper which you hand over. If the mechanic will not allow you to write it on the receipt or accept anything else written by you, then you should go home and immediately put the details of your complaint, together with a clear statement that you were paying only under protest, in writing and keep a copy of your letter. As a last resort you may have to pursue your claim in the county court and this is why it is so important to get things in writing.

Whenever you are writing letters of complaint, there are a few rules to remember which will make things easier for you. Always keep copies of letters and any other documents, and make sure that all letters of complaint contain the following:

- your name and address
- the date
- the name and address of the person you are writing to
- invoice or order numbers where relevant
- the date the transaction took place
- what was agreed or said
- what went wrong, including dates (where relevant)
- what happened next
- what you want
- when you want it by
- what you will do if you don't get it.

In other words – be specific. It is no use saying 'I expect you to deal with my problem or I'll take it further', as this is meaningless. Say instead 'I want x, within seven days, or I will issue proceedings against you in the county court'.

The next stage in a claim like this is obtaining evidence of your complaint and it may again be useful to have an independent report carried out which could assess whether the repairs that you requested had in fact been carried out correctly or at all. If you were not specific about the repairs that you wanted and if your complaint is about unauthorised repairs, you are going to find it extremely difficult without an itemised bill.

It may be that your complaint is about cost and this is why it is so valuable to know what manufacturers recommend as the price of the parts and, more particularly, the length of time that certain repairs should take. If you then know how much that garage's hourly labour charge is, you will be able to work out whether the amount they are charging you for labour is reasonable or not.

Some garages charge a storage fee for cars which are not collected as soon as the repairs are carried out. Legally, you are not obliged to pay such fees unless you were advised at the time when you entered into the contract that they may be incurred. It may be that a garage will begin to impose such a charge only once they have told you that your car is ready for collection and you are refusing to collect it because of a dispute. On the other hand, you may not have specified a particular time for collection of your car when you took it for repair and as a result you may leave it far longer than necessary before going back to collect it. In such a case, the garage could not claim a storage fee unless they contacted you when your car was ready and advised you that such a fee would now begin to be imposed. In some cases, there may be a notice in the garage about storage fees. If this is the case then you will be bound by such notices. The law assumes that people read things.

Exclusion notices

If your car is damaged whilst it is in the care of the garage, they may refer you to an 'exclusion notice' – this is a sign somewhere saying that they do not accept liability for loss or damage. Such exclusion notices may not necessarily be legally enforceable.

If your car has been damaged whilst in their care, as a result of their negligence, they cannot simply choose not to accept responsibility. Negligence, however, is a very difficult thing to prove.

Up until the late 1970s, many garages (and indeed all sorts of other service industries) displayed exclusion notices denying responsibility for virtually everything. These notices were just as legally binding as notices which advised you of storage charges and so on, and again you were expected to read them and be bound by them. In the event of some damage being caused to your vehicle, you would have had no right to make a claim against the garage if such a notice were on display.

Unfair Contract Terms Act 1977

The interesting thing about this Act is that if there is no notice at all and you have a claim against the garage, you would have to issue proceedings and persuade the court that the damage to your car was caused either by the garage or at least whilst it was in their care and that therefore they had a 'duty of care' which they had failed to exercise. In other words, you would have to prove negligence.

Now, in many ways, your case may be a lot easier if there *is* an exclusion notice displayed because the Unfair Contract Terms Act gives you the right to let a county court decide whether the notice is fair and reasonable, and if the court decides that it is not then you will have a claim for the damage to your vehicle and you will not necessarily have to prove negligence. What is even more interesting about this legislation is that in most cases when you make a claim for damages, the court would hear your side of the story and the other party would have only to 'shed reasonable doubt' for you to lose. You simply have to state your case and the onus then falls on the defendant to prove that it is 'fair and reasonable' for them to exclude liability and to prove *why* it is fair and reasonable. The court will then subject their defence to what is known as the 'reasonableness test'. If their defence fails the test, you win. It is as simple as that. What this now means is that you may be better off if a garage displays an exclusion notice than if they do not, because claiming in the county court using the Unfair Contract Terms Act is easier than trying to make a negligence claim. The majority of cases that have come to court since that Act came into force have been successful.

Here is an example of what a court might consider as fair and reasonable. You take your car to a garage, park it in their forecourt, arrange for the servicing to be carried out and say you will collect the car that same evening. Then, having locked your car and handed the keys to the mechanic you leave.

Later that day you telephone to find out whether the car is ready and when you are advised that it is, you decide that it would be more convenient for you to pick it up the following morning. The garage agrees to this but when, the following day, you return to collect your car you find it parked on the forecourt where you left it, and locked, but a window is broken and your car radio has been stolen. Naturally, you complain to the mechanic who points to a notice excluding liability. You feel that since the car radio was there when you took it in but not there now, the garage must accept responsibility and since they are not prepared to discuss the case you decide to issue proceedings against them in the county court. Using the terms of this Act, you simply point out that the radio was there and the window was undamaged when the car was taken in for repair, that you are satisfied with the repairs, but that the garage is seeking to rely upon an exclusion clause in order to repudiate your claim.

It is now for the garage as the defendant to persuade the court that their exclusion notice is fair and reasonable and in order to do so, they explain that their forecourt is open and accessible at all times; they have no facilities for locking up the forecourt, nor do they have facilities within their workshops large enough for storing vehicles. They go on to say that in most cases they try to ensure that straightforward servicing and repairs are carried out on the same day in order that cars do *not* have to be left on their premises overnight and that in this case the work was completed and you knew that your car was ready for collection.

In a case such as this it is likely that the court would decide that their exclusion notice *was* fair and reasonable on the basis that if they were unable to secure their premises at night, and this fact should have been obvious to you, it was *not* reasonable for them to accept liability for something which may happen to your vehicle whilst they were not there – particularly when you had been told that it was ready for collection but had failed to collect it.

If, on the other hand, it was possible to secure the premises at night or there was adequate space within their workshop to make sure that all vehicles left in their care overnight could be locked up inside, then it is likely that the case would go your way because they would have a duty of care.

The position remains that most exclusion clauses (in the case of services – because this does not apply in the same way where the purchase of goods is concerned) are displayed as a deterrent and cannot necessarily be relied upon. If you feel that you have a valid claim and that it is not reasonable for someone to exclude liability then it is worth pursuing your case through the courts.

It should be said that regardless of any notices, no one can disclaim liability for death or injury.

Economy

A basic understanding of how the car works will make it easier for you to understand some of the ways in which you can keep running costs down to a minimum.

Cutting costs in the short term, however, may not always be in your best long-term interests. You would not wish, for example, to save money at the expense of safety, or to pay less for oil if it meant that your engine was being damaged. You should be very wary of exceptionally cheap spares or of dubious sources of supply.

Counterfeit parts

Counterfeiting is a very common practice in all areas, and it is particularly lucrative in the motor industry.

Most counterfeit spares are produced outside the UK. Taiwan is the biggest supplier, although more recently counterfeit items have been coming from Pakistan and India, Thailand and even Syria. What is particularly worrying is that America has recently tightened up the law on counterfeit goods so that Europe and the UK may now become more vulnerable as a market for these fakes. UK legislation is, unfortunately, not as tough as it should be.

Whilst reputable manufacturers complain bitterly that counterfeiting costs them millions of pounds in lost business (and lost reputation), many consumers argue that if it is cheaper than the real thing why should they care? I have seen many examples of why we should, indeed, care very much about counterfeit car parts.

First, many fake parts pose safety hazards. I have seen brake pads which, when tested, were found to take five times as long to stop the car as the real thing. The potential danger of having these fitted to your car is obvious.

In addition to counterfeit goods, cheap parts of any kind should be viewed with scepticism and some caution. I have seen a tyre which was used on a high-performance car having been sold as suitable for that particular vehicle. The driver had a blow out on a motorway and the tyre completely shredded. It was later found by Trading Standards Officers that this tyre was, in fact, manufactured for use on farm vehicles and should never have been taken on the road, let alone be used at high speed. The driver of this car was lucky not to have been killed. The supplier of these tyres was prosecuted and all of the other tyres he had in stock were seized. However, prosecution for an offence such as this is no comfort to someone who may have been seriously injured, if not killed.

Secondly, fake parts can cause engine damage which in the long term, will work out considerably more expensive. I have seen, for example, a filter which, when stripped down, was found to be made out of a used tin can. It actually still had the label attached showing that it once contained vegetables. As a filter, it would have been effective for a very short time and even then would not have worked efficiently. I have also seen filters which are simply crammed full of old bits of newspaper. These kinds of filters will allow 'gunge' to get into your engine, and the cost of repairs when this kind of damage has been done can be enormous.

The most common counterfeit parts are filters, brake components, steering components, lights, etc. Generally, the kind of parts which are easily bought over the counter and fitted by motorists themselves. Other parts such as fuel gauges have also been found in the market place, and it has to be remembered that some dealers may be very tempted to buy cheap batches when they are offered.

Safe economy

Let us now examine some of the ways in which you can economise safely. Most of the things we shall look at are basic common sense but there will also be a few tips which are not generally known.

Tyres

As we have been talking about tyres we may as well start there. I have already mentioned 'remould quality' and explained the difference between these and true remoulds, and we have also said that radials have a longer life than crossplies. In addition, radials may also keep your fuel consumption down a little, particularly if you drive regularly on winding roads, because of their better grip.

Correct tyre pressure is not just sensible in terms of safety, it can also increase the life of your tyres. Always follow the manufacturer's recommendations and remember to adjust the pressure for motorway driving. Too much air in the tyre will make the car feel as though it handles better but it will reduce roadholding ability and could be especially dangerous in the wet. Too little pressure will make the car heavier to handle, thus using more fuel, and wear out the tyres more quickly.

Ensure that wheels are correctly balanced, and also be sure that there are not steering faults which will cause uneven wear. Remember that tyres must legally have a minimum of 1 mm of tread over the whole width of the tyre.

Driving at high speeds increases wear, especially when cornering, heavy acceleration or braking will obviously reduce the life of your tyres. Tyres wear out almost twice as fast at 70 mph as they do at 40 mph.

Careful driving saves money. You should avoid hitting kerbs or going too fast over bad roads. Hitting kerbs damages wheels, geometry and tyres and such tyre damage can cause punctures. If the geometry of the car is thrown out, uneven tyre wear will result.

When buying tyres, choose a reputable make and a supplier who will fit and balance free of charge. If you are buying new tyres, ensure that they are wrapped because rubber deteriorates if it is badly stored and the wrapper can help to slow down the deterioration.

Once fitted, give the new tyres a chance to run in. You should not exceed 50 mph for the first 100 miles.

Oil

Cheap oil is false economy.

Oil is designed to lubricate the engine and so reduce the wear on the parts. The 'viscosity' of the oil is its resistance to flow, so the higher the viscosity, the thicker the oil. However, if it is too thick it will hamper the engine movement and if it is too thin it will not provide sufficient lubrication. Poor quality oil may leave deposits which can cause excessive wear. Probably the only way to save on oil is to look out for bargain prices which are usually only available when buying in bulk.

Engine oil requirements vary according to the season. Oil gets thinner when hot. Multi-grade oils are less affected by temperature changes and so may be useful but they are not suitable for all engines. Following the manufacturers recommendations is the best way to ensure that you are using the correct oil for your particular engine temperatures.

Change oil regularly, especially if you do a lot of short journeys or drive in heavy traffic, and never let the oil level go below the minimum.

Use the choke as little as possible and do not leave it out any longer than necessary – if your fuel mixture is too rich neat petrol will remove the oil from the cylinders and cause engine wear as well as reducing efficiency. Some cars are fitted with automatic chokes, over which we have little control. They will assist starting but are generally uneconomical. Ensure that automatic chokes are always correctly adjusted.

Petrol

The mixture of petrol and air which is taken into each cylinder is compressed and the extent to which it is compressed is called the compression ratio. This ratio is what determines the octane rating of the petrol required to run the car efficiently. Petrol is given star ratings and the following is an indication of the correct star rating for the compression ratio:

Star	2	3	4	5
Octane	90 +	94–96	97–99	100 +
Compression ratio	7.5:1	8.2:1	up to 9:1	over 9:1

If petrol with too low an octane rating is used, 'pinking' will occur. This is a dull knocking sound when the engine is labouring. There may also be 'pre-ignition'. This is when the engine runs on after the ignition has been switched off.

Your engine can be damaged by using petrol with too low an octane rating, although it may be worth experimenting with a lower grade or including just a couple of gallons of lower grade to that recommended by the manufacturer. If the engine runs smoothly, with no pinking, then this could be a way of keeping running costs down without harming the engine. It has been estimated that over half of all car engines will run perfectly well on three-star petrol.

If the engine is a bit elderly, however, or in poor condition you may need a higher grade fuel.

The best fuel economy can be achieved in two ways. First, ensuring that the engine is operating at maximum efficiency. This means it should be kept in good condition, the timing and carburettor should be correctly adjusted and the plugs kept clean. The second way to cut petrol consumption is by careful driving and an understanding of the things which increase petrol consumption.

Avoid too much use of the choke, unneccessarily fast driving or acceleration, and try to select routes which keep you out of heavy traffic – stops and starts at low speeds (8–10 mph) will use up to 100 per cent more fuel. Steep hills also use more fuel. The best driving conditions are long runs at even speeds.

Do not overload the car, the heavier it is the more power it will need to move it, and distribute loads as evenly as possible (this will also help to reduce tyre wear). Towing uses a great deal more fuel and even the weight of an empty roof rack will increase the consumption so remove it when it is not needed.

Where and when you buy petrol can be important. One obvious tip is to look for discounts, but did you know that pertol goes off if it is stored for too long? So you should fill up at a busy station with a high turnover. Another useful tip is never fill your tank when a tanker is filling the pumps. Rainwater gets mixed with petrol during delivery – this is unavoidable and generally will not affect the petrol in your tank. This is because the water sinks to the bottom, but whilst the pumps are being filled, and for a short time afterwards, the disturbance in the pumps causes the petrol and water to be mixed up and the chances are that you will get quite a lot of water in your tank. Apart from getting short measure and effectively paying for water, if the water contamination is high, you will not get very far before having to have your tank drained and possibly other pricey repairs too.

Finally, always try to park in the shade on hot days. This makes getting back into the car more comfortable but it can also save fuel because petrol evaporates when it gets hot.

Servicing

The best possible way to save here is to do it yourself. Some cars though are harder to service than others so choose one which is easy. This way, even if you do have to pay someone else to do it, the labour costs can be kept to a minimum.

It is worth checking the manufacturer's recommendations regarding the time between services as well as the time taken for certain jobs. The cost of parts varies enormously too. Some spares for foreign cars may be up to 20 per cent more expensive than for a similar British car.

As your car gets older, repair costs will naturally increase and they will be at their highest when the car is between four and six years old (or between 45,000–65,000 miles). However, if the car has been badly driven or poorly maintained it may start needing major repairs long before that.

Insurance

Details of the different types of insurance available are to be found on page 16. However, insurance prices do vary and shopping around is a worthwhile exercise although it is not necessarily a good idea to change insurance companies every year. Find the cheapest and stay with them.

A variety of factors will influence your insurance costs. These are where you live, the type of vehicle you are driving and your personal details. Other factors like whether the car will be kept garaged will also be taken into account.

Some insurance companies offer discounts for people in certain jobs and it may be worth checking through your employer or union or any trade association which you may belong to.

Advanced drivers are also considered by some insurance companies to be a far better risk and up to a 20 per cent discount can be obtained from some insurance companies by people who have passed the advanced driving test (for more details see page 37).

Garaging

As we have already said, if your car is kept in a garage this will affect your insurance cost but it will also help to increase the life of your car.

Corrosion is one of the most difficult problems to correct once it has set in. Your car will fail an MOT test if it is badly corroded and it may also affect insurance claims. Insurance companies may not agree to meet all the cost of repairs to a vehicle which was in a poor condition to begin with.

Where you live can have a major effect on the bodywork of your car. If you live very close to the sea the extra salt in the atmosphere can have a damaging effect on paintwork. If you live close to certain types of industrial areas, for example a cement works, lime and other particles carry in the air and if they settle on your car they will damage the paintwork.

Never park your car under a tree which sheds sap or other corrosive materials. In fact, try to keep your car under cover as much as possible and in a garage which is not damp.

Economy checklist

In conclusion, savings can only really be achieved by good regular maintenance and careful driving. But what are good driving techniques? Here are a few hints:

- gentle acceleration and braking

- not too fast round corners and position the car correctly

- select the correct gear, never start in second. Change to top gear as soon as necessary.

- if you have overdrive, engage it only at the correct speed

- keep your foot off the clutch until it is needed

- when the clutch is needed press down firmly and release slowly

- never rev the engine when starting and do not wait for the engine to warm up before moving

- only use the choke when it is needed and return it as soon as possible

- keep speeds down so that you do not have to keep braking and accelerating

- keep a close watch on your instruments

- never continue driving when the oil light shows or the temperature dramatically increases

- warm the car up gently in cold weather

- if stuck for long periods in heavy traffic jams in hot weather switch the engine off

- avoid hitting kerbs and holes in the road.

And good maintenance?

- maintain correct tyre pressures and good tread depth

- make sure tyres are wearing evenly; if not, deal with the cause

- keep all fluid levels correctly maintained – oil, water, brake fluid, etc

- remember to put in antifreeze *before* temperatures drop

- service the car at the correct intervals – do not wait for something to go wrong

- if something needs attention do not wait until the normal service time
- keep the engine clean and change the oil regularly
- do not park in bright sunlight or under trees which shed
- protect bodywork with regular cleaning and good quality polish
- check rust spots immediately with a recommended treatment
- check brakes for wear and replace as soon as necessary
- do not overload the car or carry unnecessary weight

Insurance Claims

Whatever kind of insurance cover you have, you are obliged to notify your insurance company in the event of any accident. You may not necessarily be wanting to make a claim on your insurance for any damage, but if you fail to notify the insurance company that you have been involved in an accident, it could affect any future claims that you may have.

What to do after an accident

If you are involved in an accident the first thing to do is to get the registration number of the other vehicle or vehicles involved. Next, get names and addresses of any witnesses. You can then go back to the other party involved and get the rest of the details. It is important to do things in this order because the driver of the other vehicle may not wait around long enough for you to obtain all of the details that you need and if you are left without even the registration number of the vehicle, you will have difficulty in claiming for the damage to your car. The point about obtaining witnesses is that no matter how apologetic someone may be at the time of an accident, it could be a very different story when the other driver completes an accident report form. Very often insurance companies are totally dependent upon witness reports in making a decision about blame.

I have come across a case where a man reversed into the front of another driver, apologised profusely at the time of the accident (thereby admitting liability) and the details were exchanged. Nobody bothered to obtain witnesses. When my client made his claim, he was advised by his insurance company (he was only insured for third party, fire and theft) that the other driver had alleged on his claim form that my client had run into the back of him. This was a complete fabrication but in the absence of any witnesses, the insurance companies are in a very difficult position if both of the accident claim forms say something completely different. They will be left only examining the balance of possibility.

Notifying the police

You are not legally obliged to report an accident to the police unless someone is injured. In the event of an injury, failure to report the matter is a criminal offence for which you can be prosecuted.

You may decide that it is a good idea to notify the police if there is a dispute at the time of the accident. In most cases, if you telephone the police at the time of an accident the first thing they will ask you is whether anyone was injured. If the answer is no they will be unlikely to show any interest at all. If you are in real difficulty, one way to ensure that you get a policeman at the scene of the accident is by advising them that the vehicles are causing an obstruction and that you are not going to move them until a policeman arrives. This should produce the desired result relatively quickly! The time when you may particularly want the police at the scene of the accident is if you suspect that the other driver is under the influence of alcohol, that the other vehicle is in an unroadworthy condition, or that there are suspicious circumstances.

In the event of one of the parties being breathalysed and found to be over the limit, any subsequent insurance claim that they make may be affected.

If anyone is injured

You must stop and produce your insurance certificate and provide details about yourself to anyone else involved in the accident who has reasonable grounds to ask for them, and in particular, the police. If the police are not called to the accident you must report it, in person within 24 hours. If you do not have your insurance certificate available at the time of the accident or when you report the accident, you will be given notice to produce it within seven days. You can produce the certificate at a police station of your choice, or if the vehicle is not yours it is possible to arrange for someone else to produce the certificate for you. No matter how minor the injury appears at the time, reporting it is vital. This is not necessary if you, the driver are the only person injured.

Injury or damage to property or animals

If you cause damage to another vehicle or any other property or an animal, you must stop and provide your name and address, and the name and address of the owner of your vehicle if it is not yours, and the registration number. This information must be given to anyone who has reasonable grounds to request it. If you are not prepared to, or are unable to give the information then you must report the accident in person to the police within 24 hours. Failure to comply with these provisions is an offence the penalty for which is a fine of up to £1,000 and your licence will be endorsed.

Terminology

- *stop* means that you must remain at the scene of the incident long enough to enable anyone else involved to obtain your particulars

- *property* covers other vehicles, lamp posts, road signs, houses, walls, trees, flowers, crops and so on

- *animal* covers cattle, horses, mules, sheep, pigs, goats and dogs. It does not include cats, hedgehogs, rabbits or other similar small animals.

Exchanging details

You are not entitled to be given, or obliged to provide, the name and address of your insurance company or your insurance broker. You are only obliged to supply your name and address. If, however, you refuse to supply this information, you will be guilty of a criminal offence. It is also a criminal offence if you fail to stop after an accident.

Notifying the insurance company

Even though you may consider yourself in no way to blame for the accident, you must complete an accident report form since failure to do so would be considered a nondisclosure and can affect future claims. When reporting an accident to your insurance company, if you do not accept any liability for the accident, you should safeguard yourself by saying so. You could write at the top of the form 'for information only – I do not accept liability for this accident'.

Obtaining estimates

If you are the innocent party and wish to claim from the other person for damage to your vehicle, you should obtain a couple of estimates for the repairs as soon as possible. Remember that an estimate will not usually be the final price. The garage will list the work which needs to be done together with any parts which are required and then quote a price for labour. The cost of the parts will not be listed. Usually the estimate will say 'plus parts at MLP'. This means manufacturers' list price. In addition, the estimate will not include VAT as this will be added only when the final bill is rendered.

It is not possible for garages to quote the cost of parts because there may be some considerable delay between the time when the estimate was provided and the time when the insurance company approves the work and the repairs are actually carried out. During this time, the manufacturers may increase their prices and therefore the garage will want to allow for that.

If a number of parts are required and the final cost of the work is going to be quite expensive, the actual bill could be considerably more than the estimate once the parts prices and VAT have been added. You must remember to take this into account when you are advising a third party of any claim against them.

Claiming from the third party

The following terminology is used by insurance companies:

> first party or the insured = you
> second party or the insurer = the insurance company
> third party = any other party involved

Your insurance company may also refer to you as 'our insured'

Having obtained your estimate and reported the accident to your insurance company, you should write to the person responsible for the accident (the third party), advising them that you hold them liable and expect them to meet the cost of your damage. An example of the type of letter your should write is shown opposite.

If you are not insured fully comprehensively, your insurance broker is unlikely to help you to settle your claim and you will have to do it yourself.

Settling your claim

There are organisations who specialise in settling people's insurance claims for them and your insurance broker may refer you to one of these companies. Some insurance brokers have their own claims settling department but it should be remembered that such arrangements will cost you money. Normally they would charge a percentage of however much they recover and you will probably be asked to pay a fee and to sign an agreement to the effect that they can deduct their commission from what they recover. Before entering into any such arrangement you should consider whether or not it is worth your while.

It is relatively easy to sort out an insurance claim yourself once you understand how the system works. If you really are not able to do it on your own you could contact your local consumer advice centre or Citizens Advice Bureau who will be able to help you with your claim. Their services are free.

If you are a member of one of the motoring organisations, and especially if you are insured through them, they may also have a claims settling service.

Once you have notified the third party of your claim and supplied estimates, he or she may decide to settle the claim or to pass it to his or her insurance company. (See draft letter.) He or she must notify his or her insurance company of any claim within a reasonable time (as must you). Usually insurance companies reckon that 30 days is reasonable. If they are not notified within that time, they may refuse to meet any claims unless you can show good cause for the delay; for

Your address

Date

Name and address
of Third party

Dear Sir

Re: Accident (Date of accident).

I refer to the above accident for which I hold you
entirely responsible.

I have obtained two estimates for the cost of
repairs to my vehicle and enclose copies of them.
Please note that the estimates do not include the
cost of materials or VAT and that these will be in
addition to the amounts estimated for labour.

If your insurance company is to meet this claim I
assume you have already submitted a claim form, in
which case could you advise me, by return post, of
the name and address of your insurance company and
either the claim number or your policy number.

Yours faithfully

Draft letter notifying third party

example, if you were in hospital following the accident. You can see that any reasons for a delay must be good ones and must be genuine.

Taking a claim to court

If the third party fails to settle the claim or to notify his or her insurance company your only course of action is to take him or her to court for the cost of your repairs. Provided the claim is for less than £5,000, taking a case like this to court is relatively simple and you can do it without the help of a solicitor. Such a claim would be taken to the county court and it is so common that county courts have a special form for it. The claim is called 'Damages arising out of a road accident caused by the defendant's negligence'. (More information on claiming in the county court can be found on page 115.)

If you are going to have to take your claim to court, try to obtain as much evidence and information as possible in order to help the registrar make a decision. If there were any witnesses, obtain statements from them. It may not be necessary for them to appear in court if they are prepared to provide written statements. Take photographs of the scene of the accident and measurements of the road as well as a note of any signs or road markings. Prepare a clear and detailed sketch of what happened; and photographs of the damage to your vehicle would also be useful.

A county court registrar is only human and sometimes it can be very difficult to decide upon liability. Photographs of the damage to the vehicle can give a surprising amount of information about the type and direction of impact. Anything which you can provide in order to help the registrar make a decision will be to your advantage.

Letting the insurance company settle

If you are insured fully comprehensively, you need only complete an accident report/claim form and leave it to your insurance company to do the rest. It is important to ensure that the information given is correct and truthful. Any discrepancies may be grounds for the insurance company not meeting your claim.

On receipt of your claim, they will request details of the insurance company from the third party. Both companies will examine your respective sides of the story and then decide who they consider to be liable. If your insurance company accepts your side of the story and the other party's insurance company does too, the cost of your repairs will be paid for initially by your own insurance company who will then be reimbursed by the third party's insurance company.

If the insurance companies cannot agree on liability, or if the third party fails to notify his or her insurance company, your insurance company will still pay you for the damage to your vehicle (if you are fully comprehensively insured) and then seek to recover it directly from the third party. Whether or not they are able to do so, you will still lose your no claims bonus. Even though you may consider that you were not at fault, insurance companies are very fond of pointing out that it is a 'no claims bonus' not a 'no blame bonus'.

If the third party completes the claim form stating that you are liable and can provide witnesses and you cannot, your insurance company may pay for the damages for both parties – without informing you. That decision could be important if you are seeking to have a no claims bonus reinstated. For example, the loss of your no claims bonus may cost you more in real terms than the cost of the repairs to your vehicle. This being so you could ask your insurance company whether they would agree to your withdrawing your claim and paying for the damage yourself and having your no claims bonus reinstated. If you have a fairly high excess, you may be even more likely to want to pay for the cost of damage yourself.

It may only be when you request the reinstatement of your no claims bonus, on payment of the cost of your own damage, that you discover that the insurance company has met the cost of the third party's claim, and then reinstatement of your no claims bonus could be considerably more expensive.

If you are the one to blame for an accident, you still have the option of paying for the damage yourself. In any event, you are still obliged to notify your insurance company that the accident has taken place. The reason for this situation is that you (the insured) have a contract with your insurance company, who is obliged to meet only claims for accidents advised by you. If it were any other way, it would be possible for someone to find out the name and address of your insurance company, write to them making a completely fictitious claim against you and receive payment without your ever finding out about it until your insurance fell due for renewal, at which time you would be notified of the loss of your no claims bonus. Obviously such a situation would be fraud, but it would be very difficult to put things right long after the event.

You are obliged to report any damage you cause in an accident which does not necessarily involve a third party, for example, if you skid and demolish a lamp post or if you plough into a farmer's field on a dark night. It is particularly important to report these kinds of accidents to your insurance company otherwise you might find yourself in receipt of a bill from the local authority for a new lamp post – an extremely expensive item! Failure to report this kind of damage is also a criminal offence.

Personal injury

Legally, you have three years within which to submit a claim for damages arising out of a claim for personal injury (provided of course that details of the accident were notified to the insurance company immediately following the accident) and because of this, insurance companies may withhold a no claims bonus for a period of three years. For example, if you were involved in an accident which was your fault and someone sustained a minor neck injury, the injured party may have no intention of making any claim as the injury was minor and not worth worrying about. However, it may be that some time after the accident, they experience pain or other symptoms and they would be entitled to make a damages claim against you for any consequential suffering which they experienced.

In the event of a personal injury where anyone has to go to hospital, you will be liable for additional costs, including ambulance charges. You will receive a bill for these costs and you should pass the bill to your insurance company immediately.

If you have sustained an injury in an accident which is not your fault, you should consult a solicitor immediately. Such claims can be quite difficult to handle and you should not attempt to do so on your own.

Removal of vehicles

If your vehicle cannot be moved and it is causing an obstruction you should arrange for it to be towed away as soon as possible. If you fail to do so, the police will arrange for its removal and you may find it difficult to locate it when you eventually need to do so. You will also be liable for the costs involved in towing it and for any storage costs incurred from the date that it was removed until the date when you finally arrange for its removal from storage. Such consequences are supposed to be foreseeable by you and as such the police will not notify you that they have arranged for the vehicle to be towed away. This could cause considerable difficulty if you were injured and hospitalised. It may be some time before you are able to deal with whatever has happened to your car and during that time it could have incurred a lot of money in storage charges. You may also find that your insurance will not meet these charges and that you are unable to claim them from anyone else.

If your car has been towed away and is being held in a garage or breakers' yard, you should try to arrange for its removal as quickly as possible. It may be that the car is a write-off in which case you must arrange for your insurance company to send an engineer as quickly as possible in order to agree that the vehicle is indeed a write-off so that you can allow the storage company to dispose of it. You must not dispose of it until it has been seen by the insurance company's engineer. If you wait until you receive notification from your insurance company that they are treating it as a total loss, there could be a considerable delay during which the storage charges will mount up and your insurance company will not be liable for them.

Insurance companies assume that you have sufficient money lying around to pay for any repairs as soon as they have agreed the estimates. As far as you are concerned, this may not be the case and if the accident was not your fault and you are the insured third party, you may not be able to afford to get your car repaired until you have received payment from the person responsible. If your car is being kept in a garage whilst all of this is being sorted out, the storage costs could be more than the value of the car. Although some storage costs may be considered foreseeable and thus an uninsured loss which you can claim from the person who was responsible for the accident, you are expected to mitigate your losses and that means arranging for repairs to be carried out as soon as possible so that storage charges do not continue to accumulate.

Non disclosure

This is probably the most common complaint and it is when an insurance company repudiates a claim on the grounds of 'non disclosure of a material fact'.

As has been explained earlier, when insurance is applied for, a proposal form must be completed. This is the document which tells the insurance company all they need to know about you. When they receive the proposal form they will not verify any of the answers you have given since not everyone has a claim and the extra work involved in checking every proposal form that comes in would ultimately put up the cost of insurance. As soon as you make a claim, however, the details on the claim form will be compared with those on the proposal form and if they are not the same (unless the insurance company has been informed of any changes in the meantime) they may repudiate the claim on the grounds of non disclosure.

If you have had accidents or convictions for motoring offences which you did not put on the proposal form the insurance company will find out in the event of a claim. Although those offences would not necessarily have put up the cost of your insurance, they will have affected the risk and therefore the insurance company is entitled to know about them. If something occurs after you have taken out the insurance, you are expected to tell the insurance company about it, if not immediately then certainly when you renew.

You must also ensure that the details on the log book are correct. For example, there is usually a question such as 'are you the owner of the vehicle?' on the proposal. If it is not registered in your name (perhaps your spouse or partner registered the vehicle for you) then you must say so because if the car is stolen or written off, the insurance company would ask for the log book. If the car is the subject of a hire purchase or leasing agreement or a conditional sale agreement then the finance or leasing company owns the vehicle until you have finished paying for it and if the car is scrapped or stolen, the insurance money will have to go to the finance company as the owners.

Your broker may have completed a proposal form on your behalf and if that happened then he would have been acting as your agent at the time. It is still your responsibility to check that all the information on the form is correct before you sign it.

Valuation

Insurance is not designed to put you in a better position than that which you were in before the loss, so that when a claim is made you will be entitled to the current value of the car. There are lists available which insurance companies use a guide to current values. The mileage, in relation to age, will be taken into account. We have already seen that the average yearly mileage which one should expect is between 10,000 and 12,000 miles so that if, for example, a car is five years old and the recorded mileage is 80,000 its insurance value will be greatly reduced. Cars over 10 years old are no longer listed (unless they have special status, ie vintage) and so can be valued only in relation to the condition at the time of the accident. The engineer who comes to inspect the car will be looking, not just at the accident damage, but also at the overall condition of the vehicle – whether it is mechanically and structurally sound, whether the tyres are in good condition as well as whether or not it has been generally taken care of. If there are mechanical faults or defective tyres, this may affect any claim that you make on the grounds that if the car had been in better condition, the damage sustained in the accident may have been less or indeed that the accident may not have happened at all. Obviously, if the car is stolen, there will be nothing for an engineer to inspect in which case it would be very difficult for you to argue any offer that the insurance company makes if you consider that your car is worth more than they are offering you.

It should also be remembered that insurance companies are only going to be liable for the actual loss you have sustained, or the book value, whichever is the lower.

If, for example, you bought a car for £1,500 and decided to insure it for £2,000 that is your choice. The insurance company will not verify its value when you take out the insurance. However, if it is stolen six months later, you will be paid the list value which could be only £1,000. It may be that you did not get a good deal when you bought it, but that is not the fault of the insurance company and if you choose to over-insure that is not their fault either – you will still get only the current value.

Under-insurance is another problem. Whilst you will be paid only the book value if a vehicle is *over*-insured, if it is *under*-insured you may get far less than your actual loss. For example, suppose you buy a car which has had considerable modifications and extras bringing the total value of the car up to £3,000. The value without the extras would be around £1,500 and so you decide to insure it for that amount on the assumption that this will keep the cost of your insurance down (incidentally, that is not necessarily the case). The car is stolen and you submit a claim for £3,000. The insurance company could argue that since you were under-insured – by 50 per cent, and their total liability is only £1,500, you are entitled only to 50 per cent of their liability – £750. This situation is not common in the case of vehicles, but it can happen so remember that under-insuring your vehicle is just as pointless as over-insuring it, with the exception that under-insuring may cost you in the long run.

If the car has been involved in an accident (as opposed to being stolen) and you do not agree with any valuation placed on it by the insurance company, you can arrange to have your own valuation carried out. This could be done by a claims assessor (you could find one in the Yellow Pages or a local telephone directory) or by one of the motoring organisations.

Remember that loss adjustors (as they are usually called when they are employed by the insurance company) and claims assessors (as they are usually called when they are working for you) are independent and therefore valuations carried out by a loss adjustor acting for an insurance company is likely to be just as accurate as any valuation you may obtain yourself.

Part payment

After you have been involved in an accident you will be asked to submit estimates for the repairs. The insurance company may tell you to go ahead and have the repairs carried out but offering only part of the cost of the repairs based on the age and condition of the car. This problem revolves around the question of current values. For example, if your car is eight or nine years old and not in particularly good condition, the cost of a new wing – parts plus labour charges (which can be very high these days) may be equal to about half the value of the car. This is not sufficiently expensive for the insurance company to decide to write off the car, but they would not consider it reasonable for them to pay the full cost of a brand new wing when you did not have a brand new wing to begin with. They would, after all, be putting you in a better position than you were in before the loss so they may instead offer to pay part of the cost leaving you to pay the rest. You may consider this unreasonable but it is perfectly legal in terms of the insurance company's liability regarding indemnity.

It may be possible for you to find a repairer who can obtain a secondhand wing, from a breaker's yard, and fit that, in which case it would be perfectly reasonable for you to argue that the insurance company is completely liable for the labour charges.

Knock for knock

Sometimes after an accident the parties involved may give their insurance companies very different versions of what happened. This could make it difficult for the insurance companies to make a decision as to who was to blame, and in order to save time and paperwork they may decide to settle on a 'knock for knock' basis. This means that each side pays for their own damage.

If this happens you should not lose your no claims bonus if you have one. You can argue that if you were not liable for the accident and the insurance company is not prepared to waste time fighting your claim, then you should not be penalised for what amounts to their lack of enthusiasm.

75 per cent – 25 per cent

As in knock for knock, the insurance companies may be having difficulty in deciding who was to blame entirely, although they may agree that one party appears to be more to blame than the other and on that basis they may decide to settle on a 75 per cent – 25 per cent basis. In this case, if you are the person accepting 75 per cent of the blame, you will lose your no claims bonus, if your insurance company accepts the lesser proportion of blame on your behalf, you should not lose a no claims bonus. If the insurance company seeks to remove it, you should argue with them.

Without prejudice

You may see this on top of letters from either side's insurance company. Often it will be on the top of a letter which tells you to go ahead and get your repairs carried out. The insurance company may not have completed their investigations but wish you to proceed with the repairs 'on your own instruction' in order to mitigate any losses. This means that you will be instructing the garage to do the repairs and therefore you will be expected to pay the final bill even though the insurance company may not yet have paid you. You should remember that the insurance company may end up *not* paying you at all and so if you do instruct the garage to go ahead with any repairs, make sure that you have enough cash to pay the bill when you receive it.

The reason insurance companies do this is because sometimes the investigations take quite a long time and they would not wish to delay your repairs any longer than is absolutely necessary because this could involve you in a further claim, for example if your car is off the road for any time and you need to hire one, or if by waiting the cost of repairs is likely to increase. They are obliged, as you are, to mitigate any losses.

Pro forma invoice

Insurance companies assume that everyone can afford to have their cars repaired as soon as they are involved in an accident. Often, this is not the case and expensive repair bills cannot be met until you have been paid. If you find yourself in this position, the insurance company may suggest that you have the repairs done and obtain a pro forma invoice from the garage. This means that the garage will bill the insurance company, not you. However, beware because pro forma invoices do not include the cost of VAT and this will be an additional expense which *you* will have to meet. If the final bill is high, the VAT charges could be expensive.

Uninsured losses

Following settlement of a claim, you may find that you are still out of pocket. For instance if you have an excess on your policy or if the third party has an excess on his or her policy, the insurance company will pay out minus the excess. If you have had to hire a car while yours was off the road being repaired or if you incurred any towing or storage charges, all of these things can be considered uninsured losses. There may even be other losses which you incur as a result of your car being off the road for any length of time. For example, if you use it for business.

All such uninsured losses can be claimed directly from the third party – not from his insurance company. This is assuming that the third party was to blame for the accident. If the accident was your fault then you will not be able to claim any of your uninsured losses since they will be entirely your own responsibility. Some insurance policies may cover you for hiring a vehicle or for towing charges but generally these are not included.

Once the claim has been settled by the insurance company, you should notify the third party of any uninsured losses which you have, and if your claim is not met, you will have to issue proceedings in the county court.

Keeping the scrap

If your car is involved in an accident and the cost of repairs is going to be so high (either because your car is quite old and therefore has a relatively low value, or because the damage is extensive) the insurance company may decide to write it off.

When a vehicle is written off and the insurance company pays you its value, the scrap becomes their property. The amount that the insurance company pays you may be considerably less than what the car is worth to you. Certain old cars may go on running perfectly happily for years and years and others may have special or sentimental value.

If you do not want your car to be written off, it may be possible for you to make an arrangement with the insurance company. You can agree the amount that they are offering you but ask to keep the scrap. The insurance company will be able to obtain an amount for the scrap – say £50, and they would therefore deduct this from the amount that they would pay you if you were going to keep the car. You may then be able to put the money the insurance company have paid you towards the cost of repairs, particularly if you are able to get the repairs carried out cheaply either by obtaining secondhand parts or by doing some of the repairs yourself or through a friend.

This is a perfectly legitimate arrangement although you must notify the insurance company well in advance if this is what you want to do, because if the car has been towed away after the accident and the insurance company knows that they are going to write it off, they may arrange for it to be broken up in order not to incur unnecessary storage charges.

Replacing the vehicle

If your vehicle has been stolen or written off you will be expected to supply the insurance company with all of the relevant documents – the log book, MOT certificate, etc, and you will also be expected to send them the keys. Once they have met your claim, your insurance contract with them is at an end and if you replace the car, you will be expected to insure it afresh. This can be infuriating if your car is stolen only a month or so after you have taken out or renewed the insurance. It may have cost you several hundred pounds to insure it and all of that money will now be lost. The insurance company will of course argue (quite rightly) that that is what you have insurance for. The unexpired portion of your insurance could be considered an uninsured losses claim which you should seek to recover from the third party.

Some insurance companies are becoming more generous about written off or stolen vehicles and will agree to transfer the unexpired insurance cover to another vehicle - usually for an additional premium so it is worth checking your insurer's policy on this.

Contents insurance

These days theft from vehicles is common and very much on the increase. In some cases, if the thief means business, there may not be too much damage to the vehicle but in the majority of cases the thief is simply an opportunist who will see something left on a seat and smash a window to get it.

If your insurance is only third party or third party, fire and theft, you will find that you are not covered for theft *from* the vehicle, but only theft *of* the vehicle. Even if you have fully comprehensive insurance, it is likely there will be an upper limit on the amount you can claim for contents and that limit is rarely enough to compensate you for the items stolen.

If you find yourself in this position it is worth checking your household contents policy if you have one. If your household policy is 'all risks' you will probably find that you are able to claim for items stolen from your vehicle. In such a case you are obliged to advise each insurance company of the other's interest. The company covering the car will pay up to the maximum allowable on your policy and the balance can be met by the contents policy.

Theft

As your car is going to be an expensive purchase and therefore a considerable asset, it is sensible to take all reasonable precautions to safeguard it. Apart from the expense of having your car stolen or broken into, there is also the matter of inconvenience. A crime prevention officer recently said to me that it never ceases to amaze him how people will spend £5,000 or £6,000 on a car (or even more) and yet they begrudge investing about £120 for a decent alarm system.

Like any other nasty occurrence, we always assume that it simply
will not happen to us – and yet the figures speak for themselves. In
1985 there were:

> 367,426 cars stolen
> 478,968 thefts from cars

It should be remembered that these statistics reflect only the cases
actually reported to the police, and while car thefts generally are
reported, thefts from cars very often are not, particularly if the
owner has been foolish enough to leave a door or window open.
More importantly, most incidents of vandalism are very unlikely to
be reported to the police and therefore there are no statistics for the
sort of damage which occurs to cars constantly – broken aerials or
wing mirrors, damage to bodywork, attempted break-ins and so on.

The risks are obviously higher in certain areas than in others and if
we look at the 1985 figures for the London area, they really are
somewhat alarming. The metropolitan police break down the
statistics into three categories:

Theft This represents vehicles which are never seen again. What
happens to them is anybody's guess but there are a number of
theories which we will look at later in this chapter.

Taking and driving away This category includes cars which are stolen
by joyriders and are very often found not that far from where they
were left – usually dependent upon how much petrol was in the tank;
others may be taken because there are one or two parts which the
thief requires and the vehicle may therefore be recovered eventually
– lacking a door, wing, gearbox or whatever; some may have been
stolen for the sole purpose of committing a crime and these cars may
remain tucked away in a garage for several weeks before being
brought out for a 'job' and then dumped.

Theft from vehicles These are all the incidents of break-ins to parked
cars which are reported.

The figures for the metropolitan area for 1985 are as follows:

theft	35,643
taking and driving away	52,433
theft from vehicles	111,701
total	199,777

The total for 1984 was 193,200.

What happens to them?

A lot of stolen cars are exported and many of the rest are resprayed and get new number plates. Some thieves, those who really specialise, employ some sophisticated tricks and many cars are stolen 'to order'. For example, a thief may steal a particular make and model of car in a particular colour, making sure that it is the same year and identical in almost every detail to another car already on the road. The thief will then get number plates showing the same registration number as the other car and fit them to the stolen car so that there are now two apparently identical cars on the road. The stolen car will then be taken to another part of the country and sold. The result is that if the stolen car should ever attract the attention of the police for any reason and they carry out a DVLC check, the car will appear to be perfectly legitimate.

Simply obtaining new number plates at random for a vehicle is much less common these days. If the car subsequently attracted the attention of the police, it would merit more than a passing interest if the policeman's DVLC check revealed that the number plate was registered as belonging to a tractor – for example.

Stealing to order

Another little trick employed by car thieves is that of breaking into scrap yards and stealing log books of cars which have just been broken up. They will be looking for the sorts of cars which are relatively young; for example, those which have been broken up because they were an insurance total loss. Obviously they are not so keen on very, very old cars – those which have simply died of old age. The thief will then commence his search for a car which matches all of the details on the stolen log book with the exception, of course, of the number plate, which is replaced by one showing the same number as that on the log book.

The only way that such a crime is likely to be detected is if the engine and chassis numbers are also checked. But since there is rarely any need to check these numbers it may not be done for a considerable time, during which time the car may have changed hands several times so that the thief is long gone. Some car thieves even file off engine and chassis numbers, although several police departments now specialise in car theft and can detect such schemes.

Theft for parts

Many of the more collectable cars are stolen for parts. The Mini, the Morris Minor and the Volkswagen Beetle are particular examples. Older models of these cars are still very popular, but in some cases parts may no longer be available or may be difficult to get so that they will be a good target for the car thief. What is more important is that older cars are much easier to get into. Modern cars have locks which are much more sophisticated than were previously used, and even where the lock was of a good quality, it will get worn with age and therefore it may not be difficult to use a similar key. The same key may even start the engine. Some cars were notoriously easy to get into and these were particularly popular with joy riders – old model Fords for example often had very poor quality locks.

Many of the newer cars, and particularly very up-market models like the Rolls Royce, the Porsche and so on, are stolen specifically to be exported. Car thieves operating this particular line in slightly used cars are very sophisticated indeed because the sale of such vehicles is big business and there are huge amounts of money involved. Many of these cars are automatic and therefore they have to be uplifted and towed away. One would imagine that such activity might attract attention, but the thieves are ever ready with a seemingly plausible explanation for the cars' removal.

Apart from taking advantage of old or badly made locks, there is a variety of other ways that thieves can get into cars, either to steal the whole car or to steal something from it.

Tools of the trade

Breaking a window has to be the favourite but some windows are much harder to break than others. Laminated windows (these are produced by sandwiching layers of glass and plastic) pose problems for the car thief though such problems are not insurmountable to the seasoned criminal.

Many of the tools readily available in garages are used by crooks. One of the most popular is a tool called a centre punch. Although not what it was designed for, it can be used by the thief to punch a hole in the window and a small clean break is all you need to give you access to the door button which will let you in without causing too much noise or attracting attention. Once inside it is a simple enough matter to start the car up.

Another useful tool for the car thief, also readily available in your average garage or workshop, is a slide hammer used for panel beating and other similar repairs. Since about 1974 steering locks have been in relatively wide use and a slide hammer can be clamped on to the steering lock in order to remove the whole thing. It can also be screwed into a lock in order to pull out the whole barrel of the lock and the engine can then be started with a screwdriver.

Finally, comes the useful little instrument that no self-respecting car thief should be without – a 'skinny minnie' or 'slim jim' as it has variously been called, is a locksmith's tool which slides between the window and door and picks up the locking mechanism. The major advantage of using such a tool is that there will be no damage to the car, damage which the car thief is going to have to repair at his own expense before he can dispose of the car. The skinny minnie used to be available only to locksmiths and other people, such as the police and motoring organisations, who may need to get into cars. Unfortunately, and despite considerable opposition from the police and others involved in crime prevention, this tool can now be fairly readily bought by anyone.

Naturally, opportunist thieves and joy riders do not wander around the streets 'tooled up', and so there is a great deal that the average motorist can do to avoid falling prey to this particular category of thief. But if somebody is determined that your car is the one they want then the chances are they will be able to get it.

Methods of entry

Duplicate keys may be used, especially on older cars with worn locks where a key to another similar model is quite likely to fit. But that is not the only method of entry. A crime prevention officer told me of a recent case where the whole lock was removed from the hatchback of a Sierra. The owner of the vehicle assumed that someone had broken into the vehicle merely to steal the contents. However, several days later the car went missing altogether and this was because the key number was marked on the hatchback lock and the thief had simply had a duplicate key cut which fitted the door and ignition. The

messsage here is that if any of the locks on your car are ever
tampered with you should have the other locks changed immediately
as a precaution.

The interior buttons which push down to lock and pull up to unlock
the car doors are particularly easy to unlock if they are of the
'mushroom' style. A plastic strip of the type used on packing cases
can be slid into the window, looped around the button and used to
lift the button up. The same trick is possible with a wire coathanger
if there is even the smallest gap at the top of the window. The newer,
flush-type buttons which are being used more widely by
manufacturers these days prevent entry this way.

Time was when car thieves were interested only in breaking into a
car if there was something of real value inside. Especially popular of
course were expensive stereo systems even though these were
difficult to remove and took time. Most thieves would be looking for
briefcases, parcels and expensive-looking leather coats left lying
around in cars for all the world to see. But my crime prevention
officer friend tells me that these days 'they'll nick any stupid little
thing that isn't screwed down or attached – anything from cassettes
to a bag of shopping'.

Deterrents

Here are ways in which we can make the lives of criminals more
difficult.

ALARMS
There are all sorts of alarm systems. Some better than others. Some
of the systems will work only when the locks are tampered with or
anyone tries to start the car, but the most popular is the impact type
of alarm where any disturbance will set it off. The advantage of this
type of alarm is that it will make a loud and unpleasant noise when
anybody tampers with any part of the car. Some of these alarms will
continue to sound until they are reset by the owner of the vehicle,
but most of them will stop and reset automatically after a certain
period of time. The disadvantage is that they can be set off by almost
any kind of impact and this can come as a terrible shock to an
innocent pedestrian who inadvertently brushes into your wing-
mirror. Some of these systems are so delicately tuned that unusually

high winds will set them off. This can be a nuisance, especially
in the middle of the night. If the weather is particularly bad you
may find your alarm going off at regular intervals throughout the
night.

Alarms can be fitted relatively easily to any vehicle. Some of them
can be set automatically when you lock the car and others have to be
set with a key to a lock which is fitted elsewhere on the vehicle. A
really good alarm system can immobilise the engine too.

It may seem reasonable to ask why manufacturers do not
automatically fit alarm systems to cars, but the problem here is there
are so many systems available. A number of extras which can be
ordered with a new car, such as radios and so on, will be fairly
standard models available with those cars. Alarm systems have not
been standardised and thus the car manufacturers would simply not
have the facilities for the service and maintenance of alarm systems
in the same way that they have for the cars they manufacture.

There is no doubt that alarms are successful in deterring the
opportunist criminal but a determined thief is unlikely to be put off
by an alarm system no matter how sophisticated it may be.

STEERING LOCKS
Steering locks have one big advantage in that they can be easily seen
by a passing thief who may simply give your car a miss when they
spot the lock. Steering locks of course will not prevent theft from the
vehicle and since this type of crime is very much on the increase,
they are losing their popularity.

PROPERTY MARKING
An excellent way to deter the car thief is to mark all of the windows
with the registration number of the vehicle. This is easily and
cheaply done and the advantage is that a car thief looking for a car
that can be fitted with new number plates and possibly resprayed as
well is not going to want to go to the additional expense of replacing
every single window.

HIDING THINGS AWAY
You may think it convenient to keep all your documents handy in
the glove compartment but doing so is good news for a thief. Stealing
a car complete with the log book and MOT certificate means that it
can be sold immediately with no questions asked. The thief can

supply the documents to the prospective buyer and has your name and address which he will give as his own.

Leaving things lying around in the car easily visible is asking for trouble and whilst it may be your dream to have £700–£800 worth of stereo equipment in the car, it probably is not worth it unless you are going to fit a good alarm and take all other reasonable steps to prevent the car from being broken into.

Estates and hatchbacks where everything is easily visible and cannot be hidden away in the boot are a particular problem. Covering things up with a blanket is not really the answer because it still tells the criminal that there is something under the blanket. These days you can buy roller blinds to fit such cars which are quite useful in hiding things left in the car.

PARKING

Where you park is very important. If you have to park your car at night then always try to park under a lamp post, or find a brightly lit street, or better still an area where there are well-lit shops and which is busy until late in the night. Unfortunately such places often have parking restrictions.

Obviously, if you have a garage use it. And I mean always use it. It is very tempting when you get home from work, if you know you are going to be going out again shortly, to leave the car parked outside and sometimes you may even forget to lock it. This is exactly what the car thief is looking for. You may not be able to claim on your insurance if your car is parked outside your house and not garaged. Most insurance policies these days ask whether cars are going to be kept garaged, and since this materially affects the risk if you do have a garage your premium will be cheaper.

There is an example of a case I dealt with several years ago:

> Mr A came home from work one evening and found that the driveway to his garage was obstructed by another parked car. He waited for a while, hooting and trying to attract the attention of the other car owner, but without success. He then asked around some of his neighbours to see if they knew who owned the car which was in his way, but this was no use either.

Eventually Mr A went indoors and from time to time looked out of the window to see whether the offending car had been moved. The third time he looked out of the window the offending car had gone, but so had his!

Naturally Mr A immediately reported the matter to the police and to his insurance company.

The insurance company refused to meet his claim on the grounds that his vehicle should never be left outside his house unless it was in the garage. When Mr A protested bitterly that he was completely unable to garage his car because of the one causing the obstruction, he was simply told that he should have phoned the police in order to arrange for the obstructing vehicle to be removed.

Whilst this sounds like a completely unreasonable attitude on the part of the insurance company, it should be said that this is a very well-known and well-used trick. If a car thief is interested in a particular vehicle and knows where he can find that vehicle, he will deliberately obstruct the owner's garage in order to make it easier to steal the car. In some cases owners have been guilty of leaving the car unlocked and with the key in the ignition while they wandered around looking for the owner of the obstructing vehicle.

Insurance companies are within their rights to refuse to meet such claims since they will argue that garaging the car when at home is a condition of the contract for insurance and if you fail to do so, you are in breach of that contract and thereby invalidate it.

Another very common type of theft, and one which causes considerable distress, is the theft of luggage from cars.

Often, when people are going on holiday and have an early start in the morning, they may load the car with luggage the night before. By the same token, when they arrive home from their holiday late and tired, they may decide to unload the car the next morning. From a thief's point of view this is one of the best deals they are likely to get. Seldom will an opportunist thief find so many goodies in one car at one time.

No matter how much earlier you may have to get up or no matter how tired you may be, always load your car immediately before you

go and unload it as soon as you get back. It is also worth
remembering that while you are loading the car you should not leave
it unattended. It is very common for someone to leave the boot open
with a suitcase in it while they go back inside to get another suitcase.
If you are unable to leave someone with the car then lock it each
time. Never ever leave your car unattended and unlocked
particularly when it has luggage in it or any other valuables, even
if you are only leaving it for a second. That is all a thief needs.
There have been incidents of theft from vehicles in garages when the
owner is simply filling up with petrol and has just gone in the shop to
pay.

Probably the most ideal setting for the car thief is the station car park
or side road next to a tube station. People who drive part of the way
to work and leave their cars in such places regularly, get into a
routine – they like to leave their car in the same place every day. Car
thieves watch car parks and side roads and soon get to know which
cars are regularly left. From the villian's point of view he knows that
he can do what he likes to the car at his leisure because he has all day.
He is likely therefore to remove wheels, wings, even engines and
gear boxes and again you may not be covered by your insurance.
Private property, such as railway car parks, private roads and
undesignated roads are quite often excluded from insurance policies.

In the weeks before Christmas, thieves go shopping too and they
take the best advantage of the pressure which most shoppers are
under during the Christmas rush. It is very common for people to go
from shop to shop, loading their shopping into the car and then
leaving it while they go to another shop. These days, thieves do not
wait for night time or for a quiet moment, they are blatant and
daring and are just as likely to smash a car window and steal your
shopping in broad daylight in a busy high street as they are at any
other time. So either lock it away in the boot or somewhere else
where it cannot be seen.

DO

- close all windows tightly

- lock doors, boot, tailgate, sunroof – everything

- invest in a good alarm system (preferably one which will
  immobilise the engine)

- mark all of the windows
- replace old or worn locks (yale-type locks can easily be fitted)
- garage your car whenever possible
- fit roller blinds to estates and hatchbacks
- find a bright, well-lit place to park at night.

DON'T

- leave the keys in the ignition, even in your own driveway
- leave items of value in the car, even if you disguise them
- load luggage the night before or unload the next morning
- leave the car unattended, even at service stations
- leave young children or pets in the car so that you need to leave the window slightly open
- park in the same place day after day (station car parks or side streets)
- leave your documents in the car.

Motoring and the police

Ever since mechanical vehicles took to the road, there have been various Acts of Parliament regarding the use and speed of such vehicles. In the very early days, there was a law which said that a mechanical vehicle must have a crew of three and that this crew should include one person to walk in front of the vehicle with a red flag as a warning and possibly to help quieten any horses. This regulation was abandoned in 1896. However, there still remain one or two fairly obscure laws and regulations which you may not know about. For example, did you know that it is an offence (in certain areas – specifically in the metropolitan area) to wash your car in the street? Did you also know that in many areas it is an offence to carry out any repairs to your vehicle in the street except emergency breakdowns? You may also not have been aware that if you switch on the engine of your car and leave it warming up while you pop back into the house, on a cold morning, you may also be committing an offence. You will certainly be committing an offence if you leave your vehicle unsupervised with the engine running and the handbrake off.

Being stopped

Under section 161 of the Road Traffic Act 1972, the police are empowered to stop any driver of any vehicle in order to check his driving documents. If you fail to stop when waved down, you will be committing an offence. 'Stop' means to stop for a reasonable time, ie long enough to exchange names and addresses, and other necessary information. Failure to do so is an offence.

When stopped, if you do not have your documents with you the officer may issue you with a form HO/RT1. This form requires you to produce your documents at a police station of your choice within seven days. You can nominate any police station which is convenient to you and the documents which are listed on the HO/RT1 must be produced. Your driving licence must be produced by you in person but the other documents eg MOT certificate and insurance certificate, can be produced by someone nominated by you. You must have the HO/RT1 with you when you attend the police station.

If, for any reason, you are unable to produce your documents within the seven days, you should go in person to the police station of your choice and ask for extra time. If you fail to do this, you may be prosecuted.

If your documents are not in order, you will be cautioned and will have the opportunity of making a statement if you wish to. You will be warned that the offence is being considered and a report will be forwarded for a decision. You should hear whether or not you are being prosecuted within about three months and you will receive either a warning letter or a summons.

Sample HO/RT1

Fixed penalty notices

On 1 October 1986 new rules came into force, allowing the police to present motorists with Fixed Penalty Notices, on-the-spot, for a variety of offences other than parking offences.

The Fixed Penalty Notices carry a £24 fine for endorsable offences and a £12 fine for non-endorsable offences.

Endorsable offences include all of those things which incur penalty points (see page 174). Non-endorsable offences are very wide ranging and include:

- not wearing a seat belt

- parking on a footpath

- various vehicle defects

- causing an obstruction

- ignoring directions

- failure to display a tax disc, etc.

Once stopped, you will be given a ticket. If stopped for an endorsable offence the officer will request your driving licence, so that the relevant number of points can be endorsed on the licence by the Fixed Penalty Clerk. The officer will give you a receipt for the licence which will substitute as a driving licence until your own is returned, following endorsement. You will also be expected to pay the fixed penalty (£24) within 28 days and the licence will be retained until the penalty is paid. If the penalty is not paid, you will receive a summons to appear in court.

If you do not have your driving licence with you, you will be given a HO/RT1, requesting you to surrender your licence at a specified police station within seven days. Unlike other circumstances where you may be required to produce your documents, you may not choose the police station.

For non-endorsable offences, the officer will give you the Fixed Penalty Notice which will include a tear-off payment slip and the penalty must be paid within 28 days. If the penalty is not paid within this time you will automatically be declared guilty, and the penalty will be increased by half again (from £12 to £18). If this amount is not paid the notice will be sent to the local Magistrates' Court for enforcement.

In the first instance you will be invited to go to the court to pay the penalty. If this notice is disregarded then the non-payment will be treated as non-payment of a fine, which means that either an arrest warrant will be issued or a bailiff will be sent to seize your goods.

If, on receipt of either Fixed Penalty Notice, you dispute the offence you can request a hearing. In this case, the Fixed Penalty Notice will be treated as a summons and a date for a court hearing will be set.

Being reported

If you are reported for any traffic offence you will definitely be given a HO/RT1. If you do not have your documents with you the report will be submitted at the police station for a decision to be made as to whether or not to prosecute you. If you are to be prosecuted, a summons will be sent through the post. In trivial matters the police generally send a warning by way of a letter.

Note: You must give your correct name and address when being reported. Under the Police and Criminal Evidence Act 1985, if the officer feels that you are giving false details he can arrest you. That would be for any offence no matter how trivial.

Construction and use offences

Let us take a brief look at some of the most common types of offences regarding construction and use (the Road Traffic Act). Obviously a vehicle must be taxed, insured and have a current MOT certificate where relevant. All of the above are absolute conditions and no 'guilty knowledge' is needed to commit the offences. It is the driver's responsibility at all times to ensure that he or she complies.

Glass

Must be maintained so as not to obscure vision. In other words it must not be so dirty that you cannot see out of it clearly.

Horns

All vehicles must have one and it must be in working order. The sounding of a horn on stationary cars is an offence (unless at times of danger from moving vehicles, eg someone rolling into you). It is an offence to sound your horn between 11.30 pm and 7 am on restricted roads (eg a road with street lights less than 200 yards apart).

Mascots

No vehicle first used after the 1 October 1937 may carry a mascot in a position where it is likely by reason of projections, for example sharp points, to cause injury to anyone with whom the vehicle may collide. Some vehicles have mascots which are spring loaded, for example, the figure on the front of a Rolls Royce. The spring loading enables the mascot to move reasonably freely on impact and to retain its original position when it is let go.

Lights

Vehicles must have properly maintained lights which must be white at the front and red at the back. It is an offence to display a white light at the rear (except when reversing). For example, if one of your rear lights has been broken, and the bulb is not covered by the red glass, you will be committing an offence. The number plate must also be illuminated.

Windscreen washers

The washers must be effective and the water reservoir must be kept full of water at all times.

Number plates

The number plates must be easily seen and not obscured either by dirt or by any part of the car for example, the bumper. They must be lit up at night and they must conform to regulation size and the spacing of letters. Certain number plates which have been personalised in such a way as to alter the spacing of the letters, may actually be illegal.

Noise

Vehicles must be fitted with a silencer and it must be in working order. It is also an offence to make unreasonable noise, for example by 'revving' the engine too much, especially at night. Excessive noise caused by a defective exhaust will also constitute an offence.

Tyres

Tyres must:

- be properly inflated (traffic patrols carry gauges and *do* check tyre pressures)
- not have any break in the fabric of the tyre
- not have any bulges in the sides of the tyres
- have a tread pattern of at least 1 mm around the whole tread
- not be a mixture of radial and crossply on the same axle.

Dangerous condition

It is an offence for any vehicle to be on the road in a dangerous condition. For example, if your vehicle has been involved in an accident and a wing is so damaged that there are sharp pieces of metal protruding, you could be committing an offence.

Use

It is an offence to open, or cause, or permit to be opened, any door of a motor vehicle or trailer on a road as to cause injury or danger to any person.

Reversing

It is an offence to reverse for a greater distance or time than is necessary, for the safety or reasonable convenience of road users and pedestrians.

Dangerous position

It is an offence to leave a vehicle in such a position that it is likely to cause danger to other persons using the road (for example, parking on a bend).

Vehicle rectification scheme

There is a scheme which is still experimental in certain parts of the country and may eventually become law. The scheme is known as the vehicle rectification scheme and it works like this.

If you are stopped and reported for a construction and use offence – in other words there is something wrong with your vehicle, such as a hole in the exhaust – there is a new option whereby you are given fourteen days' grace to fix the defect thus preventing prosecution.

The officer will (at his discretion, dependent on the nature of the offence) offer you the opportunity to take part in the scheme *after* taking the initial report. If you agree to take part, he will give you a form with the vehicle defects listed on it. You will then have 14 days within which to have the car repaired and checked at an MOT centre. The centre will endorse the form to the effect that the car has been rectified, and you can then send the form to an address which will be shown on it and no futher action will be taken regarding the original offence.

Serious offences

Any road with lamp posts less then 200 yards apart automatically becomes a restricted street and the speed limit will therefore be 30 mph unless otherwise directed.

The maximum speed on a single carriageway is 60 mph and the maximum speed on dual carriageways and motorways is 70 mph. These limits apply only if there are no signs indicating otherwise. For example, there may be signs on a motorway reducing the maximum speed limit for reasons such as bad weather conditions, or roadworks.

Some of the more serious motoring offences, covered under the Road Traffic Act 1972, carry possible prison sentences.

- section 1: causing death by reckless driving

- section 2: reckless driving. Having regard to all the circumstances. Circumstances include the nature, condition and use of the road and the amount of traffic on the road.

- section 3: driving without due care and attention or without reasonable consideration for other persons using the road

- driving not in a position to have control. A person driving a car must be in a position to have proper control of that vehicle. The person must not be hampered in any way. For example, if your vehicle is overloaded so that your vision may be obscured either through your rear view mirror or through any of the windows, or even if you were driving with a dog on your lap, you could be committing an offence.

Common offences

Section 22 of the Road Traffic Act

Failing to conform to the indication given by a lawfully placed traffic sign: red traffic light, fixed or portable, (includes roadworks) flashing lights on motorways and railway crossings; stop sign; give way sign; keep left and other directional signs; no entry; signs placed by police to indicate a prohibition, restriction or requirement occasioned by extraordinary circumstances; double line markings (white) on a carriageway.

Bus lane

It is an offence to drive in a bus lane which is indicated by a sign adjoining the lane indicating the times of use.

Zebra crossings

It is an offence to park anywhere in the confines of a crossing or overtake a vehicle on the approach to a crossing (again within the confines). Drivers must stop and allow people to cross, if any person has already stepped on the crossing itself before the vehicle reaches it.

Penalty points system

The penalty points system came into effect in 1982. Previously, the system was the 'rule of three'. This meant that if you had three endorsements within three years you would be automatically banned from driving for six months. In addition, you would have the penalty for the third offence. That third endorsement remained active for three years so that a fourth offence could mean suspension again.

The new system operates on the basis of totting up points: 12 points within three years and you will automatically be suspended for six months. At the end of that time your licence is wiped clean but if you get another 12 points over any three years then the suspension could be 12 months for the second time around. In general, the system seems much fairer until you examine more closely the question of what constitutes 'one incident'. When this system became law, it was not the Department of Transport's intention that a driver should face an aggregation of points through a variety of offences which arose out of one incident. For example, if you were stopped for going through a red light, you would incur a three-point penalty. If at the same time, you were prosecuted for having three illegal tyres (three points each), if aggregation were the rule, this would be a total of a 12-point penalty for which your licence would be suspended.

Magistrates have expressed unease about no aggregation and so it has become a greyish area, although the government is quite clear that the law says there should be no aggregation of points arising from the same incident.

The question of one incident poses difficulties in a case for example where there was a short distance in time between being stopped for one offence and questioned about another. Could this constitute two different incidents?

Scoreboard

Offence	*points*
Driving without a licence	2
Failing to comply with conditions of licence	2
Driving with uncorrected defective eyesight	2
Refusing to submit to a test of eyesight	2

Driving while disqualified as under age	2
Speeding, pedestrian and traffic regulations (each)	3
Contravention of pedestrian crossing regulations	3
Failure to obey a sign exhibited by school crossing patrol	3
Contravention of order prohibiting or restricting use of street playground by vehicles	2
Taking or attempting to take conveyance without consent or lawful authority or driving or attempting to drive a motor vehicle so taken or allowing oneself to be carried in a motor vehicle so taken. Going equipped for stealing with reference to theft or taking a motor vehicle	8
Stealing or attempting to steal a motor vehicle	8
Failing to comply with traffic directions	3
Leaving vehicle in a dangerous position	3
Contravention of construction and use regulations	3
Contravention of traffic regulations on special roads	3
Careless or inconsiderate driving	2–5
Failing to report or give particulars of an accident	4–9
Failing to stop after an accident	5–9
Driving while disqualified by order of a court	6
Using, or causing or permitting use of, a motor vehicle uninsured and unsecured against third party risks	4–8
Taking (in Scotland) a motor vehicle without consent or lawful authority, or driving or allowing oneself to be carried in a motor vehicle so taken	8
Reckless driving	10
In charge of a vehicle when unfit through drink or drugs	10
Being in charge of a vehicle with an alcohol level above legal limit	10
Failing to provide a breath test specimen	4
Failing to produce specimen for analysis	10

Note: Although a 10-point offence, drunken driving still carries automatic disqualification for 12 months or more. Furthermore, although reckless driving also carries only a 10-point penalty, it is an offence which may carry a prison sentence in certain circumstances as we have already seen.

Wheel clamps

Wheel clamps (also known as the Denver Shoe, after the town in
America where they were first used) are an effective method used in
many parts of the country to penalise motorists who park illegally.

The clamp is fitted to the wheel in order to prevent the car
being driven. The clamp can only be unlocked by the police and this
will only be done after the driver has been to the appropriate
police pound and paid the parking penalty plus the unlocking fee
and any other fees which may have been associated with the illegal
parking.

The clamp has been found to be extremely effective. It is a much
cheaper method, as far as the police are concerned, than towing away
a vehicle to a police pound and motorists are not just subjected to
heavy financial penalties, but they are also put to considerable
inconvenience and some humiliation. Once you have paid all of your
penalties, you must go back and wait with your car until an officer
arrives to unlock the clamp. This in itself is humiliating and, what is
worse, the police are deliberately slow in de-clamping the vehicle
(the average time is between three and four hours). The driver is
deliberately kept waiting as a further deterrent.

You may be interested to know that in some areas companies have
been formed offering a de-clamping service. They cannot unlock the
clamp for you but what they will do is arrange to go and pay your
penalties, return to your car and wait until the officer arrives to
de-clamp it, and then take your car home for you. The fees they
charge for this service are fairly high, but many drivers consider that
the convenience factor is well worth the money. There are also clubs
which you can join, paying an annual membership, who will also
offer this type of service. You will of course have to pay all of the
penalties and costs involved in addition to your annual membership
but, again, many motorists may consider that the costs are a good
investment.

Parking tickets

If you park illegally and incur a parking ticket, you will be committing an offence if you interfere with the ticket in any way. It is also an offence for an unauthorised person to remove a parking ticket from a vehicle. The ticket will show the registration number of your vehicle, the place where it was seen illegally parked, the time and date of the offence and it will also show the number of the type of offence being committed.

If you are in any doubt about the offence, the details will be shown on part 3 of the parking ticket which lists the numbered offences to which the parking tickets apply – for example 'the vehicle was waiting in a restricted street – in a parking zone'.

When you receive a parking ticket, you have an opportunity to pay the penalty within 21 days of receiving it. The address to which you must send the penalty will be shown on the ticket. If you pay the fixed penalty, the offence will be discharged and you will not be prosecuted.

If you do not pay the penalty within the stated time limit, you will be sent (by recorded delivery) a 'notice to owner of vehicle'. This notice will detail the offence which has been committed and you will have to complete and return it within 14 days.

You will still have an opportunity to pay the fixed penalty but if you fail to do so and if you fail to return the notice, you will be committing an offence for which the maximum fine is £400.

Drinking and driving

According to a consultative document issued by the Department of Transport 'drinking and driving is one of our most serious road safety problems. It is the cause of some 1,200 deaths each year. This is about one in five of all deaths on the road. One in three of all drivers killed have more than the prescribed limit of alcohol in their blood. At night the proportion is two in every three.'

The breath test was introduced by the Road Safety Act 1967 and the alcohol limit was set at 80 milligrammes per 100 millilitres of blood.

The following are offences under the Transport Act 1981:

- drunken driving or driving with excess alcohol. Penalty: disqualification for a minimum of 12 months and up to a £2,000 fine and/or 6 months' imprisonment (the blood alcohol level is taken into account when fixing disqualification period).

- refusing evidential specimen (driving). Penalty: disqualification for 18 months; up to £2,000 fine and/or 6 months' imprisonment.

- in charge drunk or with excess alcohol or refusing evidential specimen. Penalty: endorsement of 10 penalty points; fine of up to £1,000 and/or 3 months' imprisonment.

- refusing roadside breath test. Penalty: endorsement of 4 penalty points. Fine of up to £400.

In 1983 the roadside Intoximeter came into effect. The introduction of the Intoximeter means that alcohol levels are now measured as microgrammes in a 100 millilitres of breath. Offenders have the option of a blood test or, under certain circumstances, a urine test in addition to the Intoximeter reading.

Equivalents:	Blood	Urine	Breath
Legal limit	80 mg/100 ml	107 mg/100 ml	35 mg/100ml
	150 mg	200 mg	66 mg
	200 mg	267 mg	88 mg
	250 mg	333 mg	110 mg

The more you drink, the higher will be the maximum of blood or breath alcohol concentration, but there are a number of other things which you should take into account. For example, what you drink is important. Drinks with about 20 per cent alcohol by volume such as sherry or gin and tonic are most rapidly absorbed into the blood. Less concentrated drinks such as beer or cider are absorbed more slowly. The slower the rate of absorption the lower the maximum blood/breath alcohol concentration.

Your body eliminates alcohol at a rate of approximately a single measure of spirit or half a pint per hour. So if you are drinking at a greater rate than that there will be an increased quantity of alcohol in the body.

The assumption that drinking on an empty stomach is more likely to make you drunk is of course quite true. Food in the stomach, especially fatty substances, slows down the absorption of alcohol. Your weight will also have an effect on the alcohol concentration. Alcohol, once absorbed, is distributed by the blood and mixes with water in the body. As our bodyweight is nearly two-thirds water, a lighter person, with less water in the body, will reach a higher blood/alcohol level for a given consumption that would a person who was much heavier.

Generally, women have proportionately more fatty tissues than men of similar weight and so for the same amount of drink they will reach a higher blood/alcohol level.

Alcohol levels cannot really be estimated reliably but the Transport and Road Research Laboratory produced the following rough guide.

> For an 11-stone man drinking one pint of beer (two 'units') quickly on an empty stomach, the alcohol content of his blood will rise to a peak of 30 mg/100 ml after about an hour; it will then reduce at the rate of one 'unit' (half a pint of beer) per hour. Another pint drunk quickly after two hours will again increase the level.

The rate at which alcohol is eliminated from the body, however, is slightly more predictable at one 'unit' per hour so that the only sure guide is to calculate the number of hours elapsed after the time of drinking. Even so, it may be a very long time before the blood is completely free of alcohol and someone who has drunk very heavily one night until quite late, could still be over the limit when driving to work the next morning.

As an indication of 'units' the following guide may be useful, each of these is the equivalent of one 'unit' of alcohol:

- half a pint of ordinary beer or cider
- a third of a pint of strong beer
- one glass of wine
- one glass of sherry
- one single measure of whisky or other spirits.

When we talk about single measures, we are referring to the standard English measures. Scottish measures of spirits are 20 per cent larger than English ones and measures in Northern Ireland are 50 per cent larger. Obviously, when drinking at home the measures are frequently more generous than any you will get at a pub.

Taking your car abroad

There are a number of things which you need to prepare for well in advance, whether it is only a very short trip – a weekend in France, or whether you intend taking your car abroad for much longer. You must be sure that you comply with all of the necessary regulations relating to the country in which you will be travelling, you must make sure that car and all of your documents are in order, and you must comply with the customs requirements when entering other countries or upon your return.

The car

The first thing you must do is to fit a GB plate. This is compulsory and failure to comply with this regulation could result in an on-the-spot fine.

The GB plate (or international distinguishing sign) must be of the approved pattern (oval with black letters on a white background) and size (GB at least 6¾ inches by 4½ inches), and must be displayed on a vertical surface at the rear of your vehicle (and a caravan or trailer if you are towing one). On the continent checks are made to ensure that a vehicle's nationality plate is in order.

Make sure that you service the car well in advance of departure and that your spare wheel, jack and other tools are all in order. It would be sensible to carry certain small spares. Especially things like a set of replacement bulbs – in Spain and Yugoslavia it is compulsory to carry a replacement set.

Make sure that your headlights are adjusted so that the dipped beam does not light the wrong side of the road and dazzle oncoming traffic.

The adjustment can be made by the use of beam converters or deflectors which are easily purchased. Beam deflectors must be used with quartz halogen lamps and it is important to remember to remove the converters or deflectors as soon as you return to the UK.

In France it is strongly recommended that headlights emit a yellow beam. Beam deflectors emit a yellow beam, but with beam converters it is necessary to coat the outer surface of the headlight glass with yellow plastic paint to achieve this. If your car is not equipped with a rear view mirror on the left side it would be a good idea to have one fitted in order to allow for driving on the right.

In many European countries, lead-free petrol is now being sold. If your car is designed to run on leaded petrol and is filled with unleaded petrol, it will not do any immediate harm, provided that it is the correct octane rating and the next fill is of leaded petrol.

You should invest in a warning triangle (of the sort which can be stood behind the car in the event of a breakdown), a first aid kit and a fire extinguisher. In many European countries, the carrying and use of warning triangle, the carrying of first aid kits and fire extinguishers are compulsory.

Insurance

You must make sure that your car insurance is up to date and that it is of the correct type. Contact your insurer at least a month before taking a car abroad.

Over the last few years, many of the European countries have dispensed with the need to inspect insurance documents at frontier crossings and all British motor insurance policies provide the minimum cover required by law in the countries which have signed the non-inspection agreement. These are Austria, Finland, Hungary, Sweden, Switzerland, Czechoslovakia, German Democratic Republic, Norway and Poland, plus the 10 EEC nations.

Although Greece, Portugal and Spain are members of the EEC, they are not a party to this agreement which means that a green card must be obtained from your insurer who will normally require at least 28 days' notice. You will have to pay for the green card.

Applying for a green card is simply asking your insurer to extend your existing cover to apply in any of the countries you will be visiting. The green card can be obtained for you by your insurance broker and you should ask what cover will be provided. Different insurance companies offer different types of cover. For example, most continental extensions will cover things like ferry journeys. If a vehicle is stolen or written off in some European countries, the authorities may demand import duty from the owner. This is covered by some policies but not all of them.

In Italy, if you are involved in a road accident you will be required by the police to produce your green card. In Spain you will also need 'bail bonds'. This is because the authorities in Spain can detain a driver and a vehicle following an accident unless a deposit is paid. The bond, which can be obtained at the same time as the green card, provides for payment of this deposit and it can also be used to pay any fine which may be imposed although you would have to reimburse the insurer.

If you do not take a green card with you when travelling to the countries requiring it, you will be required to take out insurance at expensive short-term rates at the frontier of each country concerned.

If, while you are abroad, other people will be driving your car – perhaps a relative or friend, and these are people who are not normally covered on your own insurance, do not forget to extend your policy to cover them. If your car is written off in an accident or is stolen you may find yourself having to pay import duty to the government of the country where the incident occurs. If you have arranged to have your UK comprehensive policy extended then you will be covered against this risk otherwise you will have to foot the bill yourself.

Personal and other insurance

At least six weeks before going abroad, you should have a word with your doctor regarding any vaccinations which may be needed and if you are taking any medication you should make sure that you obtain sufficient supplies from your doctor before you go. It would also be a good idea to have a dental check up.

Certain European countries have agreed that in urgent cases, free or reduced cost medical treatment will be provided but you will need a certificate called an E111. You can obtain one from your local Department of Health and Social Security office before you go abroad and you should keep it with your passport. If you need urgent medical treatment while you are away and you have not applied for your E111, get in touch with the local health insurance authorities in the country which you are visiting and ask them to obtain the form from the UK.

There is a guidance leaflet called *Medical costs abroad* (SA30) which you can obtain from your local Department of Health and Social Security. The leaflet explains what you need to know about medical treatment abroad and also contains an application form for an E111.

Do remember, however, that if you require medical treatment abroad it can be extremely expensive and if anyone needs to be brought back to this country in the event of illness or even death, you will have to meet all of those costs yourself. Therefore, it is sensible to obtain travel insurance sufficient to meet any such occurrence. If you are driving abroad, this is especially important because if you have an accident you may not be covered for any of the medical treatment which you might need. Check with your insurance company or travel agent, well in advance.

Finally, you should make sure that your personal belongings have adequate insurance. If you have a household/contents policy, which has 'all risks' additional cover, you can ask your insurance company to extend your all risks cover for the period you will be away and to cover your belongings for the countries to be visited.

Even if your motor insurance cover is fully comprehensive, it may not be as comprehensive when the car is in a different country and the amount of cover that you will have on such a policy for personal belongings inside the car will certainly not be sufficient to cover you in the event of loss of all of your luggage and other personal belongings.

European accident statement

Many insurance companies now issue their policy holders with a standard form known as a European accident statement. This means that if you are involved in an accident whilst you are abroad, you can record on the form all of the agreed facts regarding the accident without including any admission of liability. The European accident statement is being used increasingly in western Europe and as the English translation follows the format of continental versions there should be no difficulty in agreeing the facts with any others involved in the accident. If you do use this form then you should send it to your insurers together with your claim form. You would be well advised to keep copies for yourself.

Other documents

You will need to take your driving licence with you. Make sure that it is up to date. You must also take the vehicle registration documents (log book). If for any reason you do not have a log book, you should apply in person or in writing to a local vehicle licensing office at least 10 working days before you are leaving the country to get a log book.

If your vehicle is the subject of a hire purchase or leasing agreement, you will need to seek permission of the finance company to take the car out of the country.

Remember to take your certificate of insurance and the green card where required. If travelling to Spain, take your bail bonds and, finally, do not forget your passport and E111. Keep all your documents together securely but readily available.

Customs

You can obtain a booklet called *How to go through British customs* from any collector of customs and excise whose address and telephone number can be found in the local telephone directory. In the back of this booklet there are two stickers – a green 'nothing to declare' sticker and a red 'goods to declare' sticker. These stickers can be used upon your return to this country in order to pass through customs more quickly. You should display the sticker on your windscreen. The booklet also lists the current duty and tax-free allowances.

Any customs declarations apply not just to the driver of the vehicle but to each person in the vehicle, and if anyone travelling in your car has any goods to declare or if any of you are in doubt, you should display the red sticker and you will then be directed to a customs officer. If you have no more than the duty free allowances, no prohibited or restricted goods, no goods for trade purchases and you are UK residents, you can display the green sticker and you will then normally be allowed through customs with only a short stop. However, the customs officer has the right to detain you and carry out a more detailed inspection if he wishes.

In order to save time and any possible difficulties, you should keep receipts for any items such as cameras, radios and so on which were bought in this country and upon which you have already paid duty or tax and if there are any goods to declare, you should make a detailed list and also carry the receipts.

Make sure that you check which goods are prohibited or restricted or which may need an import licence. All of this information can be obtained from your local customs and excise department.

Countries' special rules

Austria

Drinking and driving If there is 0.08 per cent or more alcohol in the bloodstream, there are severe penalties including fines and imprisonment. Even drivers with a lower level of alcohol may be considered unfit to drive if a police surgeon so decides.

Driving licence The minimum age at which a UK driving licence holder may drive in Austria is 18. If you are stopped, you may need to produce your passport as well.

Fines Fines for motoring offences are demanded on-the-spot. The officer collecting the fine should issue an official receipt.

Insurance Third party insurance is compulsory and a green card is recommended.

Lights Dipped headlights must be used in poor daytime visibility. Parking lights may only be used in built-up areas if there is adequate all-night street lighting (a broad red band around a lamp post signifies that it goes out at midnight).

Passengers Children under 12 are not permitted to travel in a vehicle as front-seat passengers unless they are using special seats or safety belts suitable for children.

Seat belts Compulsory for driver and front-seat passenger and if rear seat belts are fitted, it is compulsory to wear them.

Speed limits Standard legal limits, which may be varied by signs, are – in built-up areas 31 mph (50 kph), outside built-up areas 62 mph (100 kph) and motorways 81 mph (130 kph).

Notes The carrying of a warning triangle and a first aid kit is compulsory. Hitchhiking is prohibited in Burgenland, Styria, Upper Austria and Vorarlberg for persons under the age of 16.

Belgium

Drinking and driving If there is 0.08 per cent or more alcohol in the bloodstream, there are severe penalties including fines and imprisonment. Even drivers with a lower level of alcohol may be considered unfit to drive if a police surgeon so decides. The penalty may also include surrender of your driving licence. A fine and/or prison sentence will be imposed.

Driving licence The minimum age at which a UK driving licence holder may drive in Belgium is 18. If you are stopped, you may need to produce your passport as well.

Fines Fines for motoring offences are on-the-spot. The officer collecting the fine should issue an official receipt. N.B. motorists can refuse to pay an on the spot fine; a foreign motorist refusing to do so may be invited to make a surety payment and if he does not his vehicle may be impounded.

Insurance Third party insurance is compulsory and a green card is recommended.

Lights Dipped headlights should be used in poor daytime visibility. Sidelights to be used for parked vehicles when visibility is reduced to less than 200 metres (219 yards) or at night when public lighting is not sufficient to make the vehicle visible from 100 metres (109 yards).

Passengers Children under 12 are not permitted to travel in a vehicle as front-seat passengers when rear seating is available.

Seat belts Compulsory.

Speed limits Standard legal limits, which may be varied by signs, are – in built-up areas 37 mph (60 kph), outside built-up areas 56 mph (90 kph) and motorways 74 mph (120 kph). Minimum speed on motorways 43 mph (70 kph).

Notes The carrying of a warning triangle is compulsory.

Denmark

Drinking and driving If there is 0.08 per cent or more alcohol in the bloodstream, there are severe penalties including fines and imprisonment. Even drivers with a lower level of alcohol may be considered unfit to drive if a police surgeon so decides. Severe penalties include licence suspension, fines or imprisonment depending on the amount of the excess.

Driving licence As for UK.

Fines Fines for motoring offences are on-the-spot. The officer collecting the fine should issue an official receipt. Visitors who infringe traffic regulations can expect to be heavily fined.

Insurance Third party insurance is compulsory and a green card is recommended.

Lights The use of dipped headlights is recommended in poor daytime visibility.

Passengers It is recommended that children do not travel in the front seats as passengers.

Seat belts As for UK.

Speed limits Standard legal limits, which may be varied by signs, are – in built-up areas 31 mph (50 kph), outside built-up areas 49 mph (80 kph) and motorways 62mph (100 kph).

Notes The carrying of a warning triangle is compulsory. Generally there is a duty to give way to traffic approaching from the right. A line of white triangles (sharks teeth) painted across the road indicates that you must stop and give way to traffic on the road you are entering.

Finland

Drinking and driving If there is 0.05 per cent or more alcohol in the bloodstream, there are severe penalties including fines and imprisonment. Even drivers with a lower level of alcohol may be considered unfit to drive if a police surgeon so decides.

Driving licence The minimum age at which a UK driving licence holder may drive in Finland is 18. If you are stopped, you may need to produce your passport as well.

Fines Police may impose but not collect on-the-spot fines for parking infringements. Fines are payable at a post office.

Insurance Third party insurance is compulsory and a green card is recommended.

Lights Use of dipped headlights is compulsory during the day outside built-up areas.

Passengers There are no restrictions on the age of front-seat passengers.

Seat belts As for UK.

Speed limits Standard legal limits, which may be varied by signs, are – in built-up areas 31 mph (50 kph), outside built-up areas between 37 mph and 62 mph (60 kph–100 kph), according to the quality of the road and motorways 74 mph (120 kph). Reduce speeds to between 18 and 31 mph (30–50 kph) on roads covered with gravel or loose stones.

Notes The carrying of a warning triangle is compulsory.

France and Monaco

Drinking and driving If there is 0.08 per cent or more alcohol in the bloodstream, there are severe penalties and a visiting motorist will be prohibited from driving in France.

Driving licence The minimum age at which a UK driving licence holder may drive in France is 18. If you are stopped, you may need to produce your passport as well.

Fines On-the-spot fines are severe. An official receipt showing the amount must be issued by the officer collecting the fine.

Insurance Third party insurance is compulsory and a green card is recommended.

Lights Dipped headlights must be used in poor daytime visibility. It is strongly recommended that headlights emit a yellow beam. Note: Beam deflectors emit a yellow beam, but with beam converters it is necessary to coat the outer surface of the headlamp glass with yellow plastic paint.

Passengers Children under 10 are not permitted to travel in a vehicle as front-seat passengers.

Seat belts As in the UK.

Speed limits Standard legal limits, which may be varied by signs, are – in built-up areas 37 mph (60 kph), outside built-up areas 56 mph (90 kph) but 68 mph (110 kph) on dual carriageways separated by a central reservation and 81 mph (130 kph) on motorways – there is a minimum speed limit in the fast lane on a level stretch of motorway during good daytime visibility of 49 mph (80 kph). In wet weather, speed limits outside built-up areas are reduced to 49 mph (80 kph), 62 mph (100 kph) and 68 mph (110 kph) respectively. Note: Visitors who have held a driving licence for less than one year must not exceed 56 mph (90 kph) or any lower speed limit.

Notes Warning triangle or hazard warning lights compulsory (it is recommended that a warning triangle is always carried). At signed roundabouts bearing the words 'vous n'avez pas la priorité' or 'cedez le passage', traffic on the roundabout has priority; where no such sign exists traffic entering the roundabout has priority.

Germany (West)

Drinking and driving If there is 0.08 per cent or more alcohol in the bloodstream, there are severe penalties including endorsement of driving licence, during which time the driver is banned from driving in West Germany.

Driving licence The minimum age at which a UK driving licence holder may drive in Germany is the same as for the UK.

Fines Fines for motoring offences are on-the-spot. The officer collecting the fine should issue an official receipt.

Insurance Third party insurance is compulsory and a green card is recommended.

Lights Dipped headlights should be used in poor daytime visibility. Driving with sidelights only is prohibited.

Passengers Children under 12 are not permitted to travel in a vehicle as front-seat passengers when rear seating is available.

Seat belts As for UK, but if rear seat belts are fitted it is compulsory to wear them.

Speed limits Standard legal limits, which may be varied by signs, are – in built-up areas 31 mph (50 kph), outside built-up areas 62 mph (100 kph), but on dual carriageways and motorways a recommended maximum of 81 mph (130 kph).

Notes The carrying of a warning triangle is compulsory. Slow-moving vehicles must stop and let others pass. It is considered negligent to run out of petrol on a motorway and the police can fine offending motorists up to DM 60.

Gibraltar

Drinking and driving Strictly forbidden. Nil per cent alcohol is allowed in the bloodstream.

Driving licence The minimum age at which a UK driving licence holder may drive in Gibraltar is 18. If you are stopped, you may need to produce your passport as well.

Fines No on-the-spot fines.

Insurance Third party insurance is compulsory and a green card is recommended.

Lights The use of full and dipped headlights is prohibited in built-up areas.

Passengers It is recommended that children do not travel in the vehicle as front-seat passengers.

Seat belts The wearing of seat belts is not compulsory but it is strongly recommended.

Speed limits Standard legal limit within the city of Gibraltar is 20 mph (32 kph), and outside the city 30 mph (48 kph).

Notes Warning triangles are not compulsory. The use of a car horn is not permitted within the city limits.

Greece

Drinking and driving If the level of alcohol in the bloodstream is between 0.05 per cent and 0.08 per cent it is a civil offence, if it is more than 0.08 per cent it is a criminal offence.

Driving licence As for UK.

Fines Police can impose fines but not collect them on-the-spot. The fine must be paid at a public treasury office within 10 days. You can be fined for the unnecessary use of a car horn.

Insurance Third party insurance is compulsory and a green card is compulsory.

Lights Dipped headlights should be used in poor daytime visibility. The use of undipped headlights in towns is strictly prohibited.

Passengers Children under 10 are not permitted to travel in a vehicle as front-seat passengers.

Seat belts As for UK.

Speed limits Standard legal limits, which may be varied by signs, are – in built-up areas 31 mph (50 kph), outside built-up areas 49 mph (80 kph) and motorways 62 mph (100 kph).

Notes The carrying of a warning triangle, a first aid kit and a fire extinguisher is compulsory. The police in Athens are empowered to confiscate and detain number plates of illegal parked vehicles. It is forbidden to carry petrol in a can in a vehicle.

Italy and San Marino

Drinking and driving Nil per cent alcohol is allowed in a driver's blood. Any driver 'under the influence' faces heavy fines and/or imprisonment.

Driving licence A UK driving licence is acceptable if accompanied by a translation (available at the frontier or from the AA). The minimum age at which a UK licence holder may drive is 18 if the driver does not exceed speeds of 112 mph (180 kph). If exceeding that speed the minimum age must be 21.

Fines Fines for motoring offences are on-the-spot. The officer collecting the fine should issue an official receipt. Fines will be particularly heavy for speeding and parking offences.

Insurance Third party insurance is compulsory and a green card is strongly recommended.

Lights The use of undipped headlights in towns and cities is prohibited. Dipped headlights compulsory when passing through tunnels *even if they are well lit.*

Passengers It is recommended that children are not permitted to travel in a vehicle as front-seat passengers.

Seat belts The wearing of seat belts is not compulsory but strongly recommended.

Speed limits Standard legal limits, which may be varied by signs, are – in built-up areas 31 mph (50 kph), outside built-up areas between 49 mph and 68 mph (80 kph and 110 kph) according to engine size, and on motorways between 56 mph and 86 mph (90 kph and 140 kph) according to engine size.

Notes The carrying of a warning triangle is compulsory. It is recommended that visitors equip their vehicles with a set of replacement bulbs. Failure to produce a 'ricevuta fiscale' (a special number fiscal receipt issued after paying for a wide range of goods and services including goods and accommodation) when requested to do so could result in a fine. It is forbidden to carry petrol in cans in a vehicle.

Luxembourg

Drinking and driving If there is 0.08 per cent or more alcohol in the bloodstream, there are severe penalties including fines and imprisonment.

Driving licence As for UK.

Fines Fines for motoring offences are on-the-spot. The officer collecting the fine should issue an official receipt. Unauthorised parking can result in the car being impounded.

Insurance Third party insurance is compulsory and a green card is recommended.

Lights Driving with only sidelights is prohibited. Sidelights are required when parking where there is no public lighting. It is compulsory to flash headlights when overtaking at night outside a built-up area.

Passengers Children under 10 are not permitted to travel in a vehicle as front-seat passengers when rear seating is available.

Seat belts As for UK.

Speed limits Standard legal limits, which may be varied by signs, are – in built-up areas 37 mph (60 kph), outside built-up areas 56 mph (90 kph) and motorways 74 mph (120 kph).

Notes The carrying of a warning triangle is compulsory.

Netherlands

Drinking and driving If there is 0.05 per cent or more alcohol in the bloodstream, there are severe penalties including fines and imprisonment.

Driving licence The minimum age at which a UK driving licence holder may drive in Holland is 18. If you are stopped, you may need to produce your passport as well.

Fines Fines for motoring offences are on-the-spot. The officer collecting the fine should issue an official receipt.

Insurance Third party insurance is compulsory and a green card is recommended.

Lights Dipped headlights must be used in built-up areas. The use of sidelights only is prohibited.

Passengers Children under 12 are not permitted to travel in a vehicle as front-seat passengers, with the exception of children over four using a hip safety belt and children under four using a safety seat of approved design.

Seat belts As for UK.

Speed limits Standard legal limits, which may be varied by signs, are – in built-up areas 31 mph (50 kph), outside built-up areas 49 mph (80 kph) and motorways a minimum of 43 mph (70 kph) and a maximum of 62 mph (100 kph).

Notes The carrying of a warning triangle is compulsory. Buses have right of way when leaving bus stops in built-up areas. Beware large number of cyclists.

Norway

Drinking and driving If there is 0.058 per cent or more alcohol in the bloodstream, there are severe penalties including surrender of driving licence and/or imprisonment.

Driving licence As for UK.

Fines Fines for minor motoring offences are on-the-spot. The officer collecting the fine should issue an official receipt.

Insurance Third party insurance is compulsory and a green card is recommended.

Lights The use of dipped headlights must be used in poor daytime visibility.

Passengers Children under 12 are not permitted to travel in a vehicle as front-seat passengers.

Seat belts Compulsory for driver and front-seat passengers and if rear seat belts are fitted, it is compulsory to wear them.

Speed limits Standard legal limits, which may be varied by signs, are – in built-up areas 31 mph (50 kph), outside built-up areas including motorways between 49 mph and 56 mph (80 kph–90 kph) as indicated.

Notes The carrying of a warning triangle is compulsory. It is recommended that visitors equip their vehicles with a set of replacement bulbs.

Portugal

Drinking and driving If there is 0.05 per cent or more alcohol in the bloodstream, there are severe penalties including fines and licence suspension.

Driving licence As for UK.

Fines Fines for motoring offences are on-the-spot. The officer collecting the fine should issue an official receipt.

Insurance Third party insurance is compulsory and a green card is compulsory.

Lights Dipped headlights must be used in built-up areas. Sidelights must be used when parking in badly lit areas.

Passengers It is recommended that children do not travel in a vehicle as front-seat passengers.

Seat belts It is compulsory for driver and front-seat passenger to wear seat belts outside built-up areas.

Speed limits Standard legal limits, which may be varied by signs, are – in built-up areas 37 mph (60 kph), outside built-up areas 56 mph (90 kph) and motorways 74 mph (120 kph). Visitors who have held a driving licence for less than one year must not exceed 56 mph (90 kph) or any lower speed limit. They must also display a yellow disc bearing the figure '90' at the rear of their vehicle (obtainable from frontier offices at Valenca, Vilar Formoso and Caia).

Notes The carrying of a warning triangle is compulsory.

Spain

Drinking and driving If there is 0.08 per cent or more alcohol in the bloodstream, there are severe penalties including fines and withdrawal of visitors' driving licence.

Driving licence Although Spain became a member of the European Community in January 1986 it is still not certain whether the Spanish authorities will adopt Community practice on mutual recognition of temporary visitors' domestic driving licences. Until the situation is clarified, an International Driving Permit (or an official Spanish translation of your licence stamped by a Spanish

Consulate, which costs more than an IDP) should be carried.
Minimum age at which a UK driving licence holder may drive is 18.

Fines Fines for motoring offences are on-the-spot. The officer
collecting the fine should issue an official receipt.

Insurance Third party insurance is compulsory and a green card is
compulsory. Bail bond recommended.

Lights Dipped headlights compulsory on motorways and fast dual
carriageways, even if they are well lit. Sidelights may only be used on
urban roads and single carriageway inter-urban roads provided they
are well lit.

Passengers It is recommended that children do not travel in a vehicle
as front-seat passengers.

Seat belts It is compulsory for driver and front-seat passenger to wear
seat belts outside built-up areas and on the Madrid ring road (M30).

Speed limits Standard legal limits, which may be varied by signs, are
– in built-up areas 37 mph (60 kph), outside built-up areas 56 mph
(90 kph) on second category roads, 62 mph (100 kph) on first
category roads and 74 mph (120 kph) on motorways.

Notes It is compulsory for visitors to equip their vehicle with a set of
replacement bulbs. The carrying of a warning triangle is
recommended.

Sweden

Drinking and driving If there is 0.05 per cent or more alcohol in the
bloodstream, there are severe penalties including fines and/or
imprisonment.

Driving licence The minimum age at which a UK driving licence
holder may drive in Sweden is 18. If you are stopped, you may need
to produce your passport as well.

Fines Police can impose but not collect on-the-spot fines.

Insurance Third party insurance is compulsory and a green card is
recommended.

Lights The use of dipped headlights during the day is compulsory.

Passengers It is recommended that children do not travel in a vehicle as front-seat passengers unless seated in a special child restraint.

Seat belts As for UK.

Speed limits Standard legal limits, which may be varied by signs, are – in built-up areas 31 mph (50 kph), outside built-up areas 43 mph (70 kph), but 56 mph (90 kph) or 68 mph (110 kph) on good roads and motorways.

Notes The carrying of a warning triangle is compulsory. Beware game (moose, deer, etc) as this constitutes a very real danger on some roads.

Switzerland and Liechtenstein

Drinking and driving If there is 0.08 per cent more alcohol in the bloodstream, there are severe penalties including fines and imprisonment; visiting motorists may be forbidden from driving in Switzerland for a minimum of two months.

Driving licence The minimum age at which a UK driving licence holder may drive is 18. If you are stopped, you may need to produce your passport as well.

Fines On-the-spot fines in certain cases.

Insurance Third party insurance is compulsory and a green card is recommended.

Lights Dipped headlights at all times in tunnels whether they are lit or not. Failure to do this in tunnels incurs an on-the-spot fine.

Passengers Children under 12 are not permitted to travel in a vehicle as front-seat passengers when rear seating is available.

Seat belts As for UK.

Speed limits Standard legal limits, which may be varied by signs, are – in built-up areas 31 mph (50 kph), outside built-up areas including semi-motorways 49 mph (80 kph) and motorways 74 mph (120 kph).

Notes The carrying of a warning triangle is compulsory. The Swiss authorities levy an annual motorway tax and a vehicle sticker (costing SwFr 30 for vehicles up to 3.5 tonnes (unladen) and known locally as a 'vignette') must be displayed by each vehicle (including trailers and caravans) using Swiss motorways. Substantial fines are imposed for non-display. The stickers are available from most AA centres or at the Swiss frontier.

Yugoslavia

Drinking and driving If there is 0.05 per cent or more alcohol in the bloodstream, there are severe penalties including a fine, imprisonment and/or suspension of driving licence.

Driving licence The minimum age at which a UK driving licence holder may drive in Yugoslavia is 18. If you are stopped, you may need to produce your passport as well.

Fines Fines for motoring offences are on-the-spot. The officer collecting the fine should issue an official receipt.

Insurance Third party insurance is compulsory and a green card is compulsory.

Lights Dipped headlights should be used in poor daytime visibility.

Passengers Children under 12 and persons visibly under the influence of alcohol are not permitted to travel in a vehicle as front-seat passengers.

Seat belts Compulsory for driver and front-seat passenger and if rear seat belts are fitted, they should also be worn.

Speed limits Standard legal limits, which may be varied by signs, are – in built-up areas 37 mph (60 kph), outside built-up areas 49 mph (80 kph), 62 mph (100 kph) on dual carriageways and 74 mph (120 kph) on motorways.

Notes It is compulsory for visitors to equip their vehicles with a set of replacement bulbs. The carrying of a warning triangle and a first aid kit is compulsory (two triangles are required if towing a trailer). Any visible damage to a vehicle entering Yugoslavia must be certified by the authorities at the frontier and a certificate obtained. When leaving the country, this certificate must be produced.

Selling your car

When to sell

Many people change their cars every couple of years or so as a matter of course. We have already said that because new cars often have all sorts of teething troubles in the first year, buying a car which is about a year old can be an advantage. But, in the same way, if your make of car has a reputation for reliability and trouble-free performance, such as Volvo or Volkswagen, selling it after two years can work to your disadvantage. You may have had the aggravation of teething problems without the benefits of its durability.

In previous chapters we have also looked at various aspects of depreciation. Of course, not all cars depreciate at the same rate and in fact certain cars (some of the more desirable luxury cars) may increase a little in value in the first year or so. The rate of depreciation reduces the longer you hold on to the car, but the condition of the vehicle must also be taken into account.

The best time to sell your car is before it starts needing major repairs. After all, you do not want to pay out for a big repair bill just before you put the car on the market. You will only be able to get the book value of the car, or possibly a little more depending on how you sell it, and this is unlikely to cover the additional expense of the repair. You can expect to replace your battery and exhaust every two years or so, brakes and tyres every 20,000 miles, a clutch after about 30,000 miles and so on. The major repairs tend to occur when a car is between four and six years old, assuming that it is of average mileage, say, between 40,000 and 60,000 miles.

We saw that certain times of the year were better than others if you were hoping to buy a bargain. The same thing applies when you are selling your car. December until just after Christmas is a particularly bad time for the trade and there is no reason to suppose that it would be any better for the private seller. If you can afford to hang on you would be better to wait until the spring. Somehow, when the sun shines everybody starts to think about having a car for those occasional summer trips.

We also said that selling a car just before the new registration date can be problematic. You need to remember that anyone wanting to buy a car with a new registration letter will probably be disposing of an old car. They may choose to part exchange it for the new model or they may be selling it privately, but, either way, there are going to be plenty of used cars on the market around August and September, so try to avoid these times if you want to get the best price for your car.

Preparing the car

Although you will not want to spend a lot of money on major work before you sell a car, it is worth making sure that the car looks as good as it is capable of looking. This is especially important if you are going to sell it privately because people really are influenced by appearance.

There are a number of things you can do to the basic cosmetics. Obviously, you should make sure that the car is clean inside and out, including the wheels and trims. Give the paintwork a good coat of wax polish and then turn your attention to the interior. Thoroughly vacuum the carpets and upholstery, clean all of the windows and mirrors and make sure that everything looks impressive. It may even be worth your while investing in a valet service if you cannot be bothered to do it yourself. Many garages offer this service now and prices vary around the country from about £20 for the inside only up to about £150 for the entire car – inside and out. It would be worth shopping around for the best possible price and do check whether the price includes both the interior and exterior of the car.

You may want to consider some minor repairs. Naturally you should make sure that everything is working properly – the horn, windscreen wipers and washers, lights and indicators, and replace bulbs where necessary. There may be little specks of rust that you can tidy up but beware of overdoing the bodywork repairs if you are not really competent to do them properly. It may be better to leave a little rust spot rather than to touch it up badly. Certainly if there are any really bad patches, filling them with body filler should only be done if you are sure that you will end up with a very professional finish. The car could end up looking a lot worse than it did with the rust.

If you are selling the car to a dealer it is still worth your while ensuring that it is clean and tidy because a dealer is not going to want to waste time on cleaning it up before he sells it – time is money. However, you probably do not need to go to as much trouble as you would if you were going to sell it privately. You should avoid giving the buyer any minor things to find fault with as this will only give him an excuse to try to knock the price down.

Prior to the sale you should make sure that you have all your documents to hand and that they are in order. You will have to hand over the log book and MOT certificate and leave the tax disc on display.

You must decide whether or not you are going to include accessories and 'extras' in the price. Certain things can be removed quite simply and may be worth removing but, in general, once you take something off there will be a hole or some kind of mark left and this can deter a buyer. If you advertise a car at a particular price and you intend charging extra for the accessories then you would be well advised to let any potential buyers know that, either in the advertisement or certainly when they telephone to enquire, otherwise you may be guilty of misrepresentation if you put up the price when they are ready to do business. You can always give the buyer the option of paying extra for them on the understanding that they will be removed if not wanted.

If the tax has a long time to run it will not be unreasonable for you to ask the buyer to pay something towards it.

Price

The two best ways of finding out the going rate for your car, would be looking at prices in the local, national and specialist newspapers and contacting a few dealers. Ask how much it would cost to buy a car of the same make, model and year. Then shop around a few more dealers and find out how much they would offer you for your car. The difference between what a car dealer will pay for a car and what he gets for it when he comes to sell it can be quite a lot of money and it may be worth your while selling the car privately and splitting this difference.

If you stick out for the maximum retail price of your car when selling privately you may find that it will stay on the market for quite a long time because a lot of buyers take the view that one of the main advantages of buying privately is that you 'cut out the middle man' and therefore tend to get a better deal. Generally, they will take the view that if they are going to pay the full going rate for the car then they may as well buy it from a dealer, in which case they will probably get a warranty or some other 'extras'. Of course, we know that warranties really may not be worth the paper they are written on in some cases but it is true to say that consumers get better legal protection (under the terms of the Sale of Goods Act and the Trade Descriptions Act) than they get when they buy privately. Again as a private individual you would be unable to arrange credit for the buyer. Most private sales tend to be with buyers who have the cash.

Selling privately

If you are going to sell the car yourself you will have to pay the cost of advertising it and have the inconvenience of making arrangements for people to inspect it. It may also take longer to sell. The advantage is that you will usually get more for the car by selling it this way and you will have the cash with which to obtain a discount if you are going to buy another car from a dealer.

You could advertise the car in a local paper which is likely to be the cheapest way but local advertising is obviously less effective. You really need to advertise the car as widely as possible in order to be able to sell it reasonably quickly. Advertising nationally can be much more expensive and will obviously generate a lot of enquiries, some of which may just be a waste of your time, but you are likely to get a buyer pretty quickly. You could aim for specialist publications such as *Exchange and Mart* or *Car Buyer*.

You should always advertise the car for a little more than you are prepared to accept. Buyers always expect to reduce the price and you should allow for this. On the other hand, if you advertise the car at a greatly inflated price, you simply will not get any interest in it.

When people respond to your advertisement you should arrange appointments for them to come and inspect. If more than one person is interested in buying, you should take all of their details when they inspect in case one of the buyers drops out.

Give the buyers plenty of time to have a look at the car otherwise they may become suspicious. If you are in a hurry to sell do not let them know because they may try to reduce the price. You should allow the buyer to take the car for a test drive, but *never* unaccompanied. Do not hand over any documents until the deal has been finalised and you have received payment, and do make sure the insurance cover is adequate.

You should answer any questions as honestly as you can and if you don't know the answer, don't bluff. You may find yourself accused of misrepresentation if you say something which is not true whether you know that it is untrue or not. This could give the buyer grounds to rescind the contract and claim either money back or damages.

If you know that there is something wrong with the car, although it may bring the price down it could be worth your while being honest about it. If you tell the truth, the buyer cannot come back later and ask for his money back.

Payment

Once you have agreed to sell the car you should not allow it to be taken away or hand over any documents until you have the cash. If the buyer wants to pay by cheque, ask him to arrange a banker's draft. A draft cannot bounce but a cheque can. Even if the buyer offers to pay by cheque and has a cheque guarantee card, you will not be protected. Beware especially of stolen cheque books and guarantee cards. If for some reason you are going to accept a cheque, ask to see some other form of identification and verify it. In the same way as cheque books and cheque guarantee cards, other types of identification can also be stolen. Take the cheque to a bank and ask for it to be 'expressed'. You will have to pay for this but the cheque will be cleared either the same day (if you take it to the bank on which it was drawn) or the next day. Under *no* circumstances should you release the car until the cheque has been cleared.

Make sure that you have the full name and address of the buyer of the car.

If a prospective buyer wants to buy the car but needs a little time to raise the cash, you could agree to accept a deposit, as a gesture of good faith, and wait for him or her to raise the rest of the cash. The problem with this kind of arrangement is that once you have accepted the deposit, and the buyer has agreed to buy, a legally binding contract exists and so you should turn away any other interested buyers. If the buyer then is not able to get the rest of the money together you will have lost the chance of selling the car to the other prospective buyers. This is why it is important to keep details of anyone who is interested. At the same time, you should make it clear, if you accept a deposit, that there will be a time limit, seven days would be reasonable, after which you will sell the car to someone else. If at the end of seven days the buyer is not able to raise the rest of the money or has changed his or her mind about the sale, you are not legally obliged to refund the deposit; the buyer is in breach of contract and you are entitled to claim damages for that breach of contract.

The buyer may wish to have the car inspected by someone else and may therefore suggest leaving a deposit so that you will hold the car subject to a satisfactory report. If the inspection reveals faults, then you would be obliged to refund the buyer's deposit since a satisfactory report was a condition of the contract.

The buyer of the car is entitled to a receipt for the money paid. It doesn't have to be a formal or complicated document; it only needs to contain your name and address, the details of the car, the name and address of the buyer, the date and the amount paid, and you should sign it.

You should not give the buyer any type of guarantee or make any kind of agreement in the event of anything going wrong with the car.

Selling to a dealer

A dealer is likely to offer you at least 20 per cent less than the retail value of the car to cover profit and the cost of any servicing and pre-sale checks that will be made before the car is sold to someone else.

You may get a better deal if you are offering the car in part exchange for another one. You should check on the kind of discounts available if you pay cash because if the difference is greater than you would get by part exchanging your car then you would do well to sell it privately.

Before approaching any dealers, check the going rate for your particular car and then shop around several dealers in order to get the best price.

Whilst you should go to a large reputable dealer to buy a car, the same is not necessarily true when you are selling your car. A dealer who has large stocks of vehicles is not going to want to take on too many more. Cars taking up space in the showroom or on the forecourt are costing money. If your car is a popular model which is in good condition and in great demand, you will have no difficulty in selling it to a dealer for a reasonably good price, but if your car is older and a bit the worse for wear, then you should approach a much smaller garage without a large stock currently available for sale.

You should not necessarily accept a dealer's first offer as he will probably expect you to do a little bargaining.

If your car is still the subject of a finance agreement, the dealer will want to know about this. If the car is the subject of a personal loan or credit sale agreement, you are legally entitled to sell it. However, as is explained in the chapter on credit, you may not sell a car which is the subject of a hire purchase or conditional sale agreement without the permission of the owner (ie, the finance company). Car dealers are able to check whether or not the car is the subject of such an agreement through a company called HP Information. They can get the results of this check very quickly. Under normal circumstances they would not wish to purchase a car which is the subject of a hire purchase agreement.

If a dealer does want to buy your car while it is still the subject of a hire purchase agreement, be very careful. I have dealt with a number of cases where a dealer has promised to pay off the outstanding credit and has failed to do so. Here is an example of one such case:

Mr A needed to sell his car. It was the subject of a hire purchase agreement and because he had not read the contract he did not understand that the car did not belong to him. Therefore he had not sought the permission of the finance company to sell it.

He took the car to a small local car dealer who offered him a very good price. The dealer asked whether the car was the subject of a finance agreement and Mr A told him it was. The dealer then asked for details of the agreement – the name of the finance company and the amount outstanding on the car. He then told Mr A that if he paid up the finance for Mr A he would be able to get a better deal from the finance company in the form of a discount on the amount outstanding.

The car was worth about £6,000 (retail) and the dealer offered Mr A £5,800. The amount outstanding on the finance agreement was £2,300, and as the dealer said that he could negotiate a better deal from the finance company he said that he would take only £2,000 off the price, and offered £3,800 to Mr A which he readily accepted.

A couple of months later Mr A received a reminder from the finance company that he was in arrears on his finance agreement. He phoned the finance company and explained that he had sold the car to a dealer, told them who the dealer was and that the dealer had said that he was going to pay off the outstanding balance on the agreement. The finance company then explained to Mr A that he had no legal right to do that as the car was their property and that they expected to receive all of the balance outstanding from him immediately. Failing that, they would take him to court for the balance and also report the car as stolen, which meant that he could be prosecuted for theft.

Mr A was naturally very worried about this and went to see the car dealer to find out what had happened. Needless to say, the car dealer had disappeared.

Mr A had received £3,800 from the dealer and he now had to give £2,300 of that to the finance company immediately or risk being taken to court and/or prosecuted for theft. He was therefore left with only £1,500. The car dealer, who had been able to sell the car again for £6,000, had made a profit of £2,200.

If Mr A had been unable to pay off the balance outstanding on the finance agreement immediately, and as he needed to sell the car in the first place because he needed the money that would have been quite likely, the person who subsequently bought Mr A's car from the car dealer could have been in a very difficult position. If the vehicle had been reported as stolen, the buyer would not have been the legal owner and the car would have to be returned to the finance company. In most cases, finance companies do not report cars as stolen when they are sold whilst still the subject of a hire purchase agreement. They simply seek to recover the money from people like Mr A.

Even if the dealer had still been around when Mr A went back, he would have been likely to fob Mr A off with stories such as how the cheque was in the post and so on, for quite some time. The point is that what Mr A did was illegal and so the car dealer, knowing this, could simply disregard the agreement that he had made. Of course Mr A could sue the car dealer for the money which he had had to give to the finance company but a car dealer who behaves in such a dishonest way is unlikely to be concerned about being sued. Unscrupulous car dealers quite often get sued and they will be aware that the county court system is such that *enforcing* a county court judgement is not as easy as winning your case.

We said that finance companies rarely report cars as stolen when they are the subject of a hire purchase agreement but there is a major exception to that. Here is an example:

Mr B buys a car through a finance company on hire purchase. Mr B is not a very honest man, and he needs money, so he pays a deposit and *immediately* does a 'moonlight flit' from his home address and sells the car to someone else for cash.

The finance company will write to Mr B as soon as he is in default but it will not be long before they find out that he has 'done a runner', in which case they will want to get back anything that they can.

A *private individual* who buys that car cannot be obliged to return it to the finance company. However, *if* it is reported stolen then the private individual will never obtain title, and therefore must return it to its rightful owner. This is why the finance company is likely to report the car as stolen – in order to locate it and get it back so that they do not lose everything.

When you sell your car to a dealer you should make certain that you receive a proper receipt for the money that you have paid and, like selling privately, do not hand over anything until you have the cash or the cheque has cleared.

Selling at auction

This is probably the quickest way of selling your car and will save you money on advertising and save you the inconvenience of arranging for people to inspect it. But you will not get the best price. In fact you will be lucky if you get little more than the trade price.

There may be a charge for entering the car in an auction and you will also have to pay a commission on the selling price – probably around 5 per cent. You therefore have to decide whether the advantage of being able to sell the car quickly and conveniently is greater than the disadvantage of losing a little money on the deal.

You should contact the company several days before the auction in order to reserve a lot number. You will have to complete a notice of entry, which is a form containing a variety of questions about the car, and list any major problems. You can fix a reserve price, ie, the price below which you will not sell the car.

When deciding on a reserve price, you need to know the value of your car and you should fix the reserve at just a little more than the trade value. Some companies will not accept a reserve price if the car is old – say more than seven or eight years, or if it is not worth very much. Instead, the auctioneer will make it clear that these cars are being 'sold as seen'. This way, the buyer will have no right of redress if he discovers something wrong with the car and very often dealers at auctions will buy such cars just for parts. If you are in any doubt about what sort of reserve price you should set, discuss this with the auctioneer.

The auctioneer may have an engineer who can inspect the car and would probably be prepared to give you a report on it. You would have to pay for this but it may mean, if the report is good, that you will get a better price for the car when it goes into the auction. It may also mean, however, that if the car doesn't get a particularly good report, the price will have to be reduced.

You would be well advised to attend when your car is being auctioned. It is not unknown for some of the less reputable auctioneers to tell you that the car was sold for less than it actually was sold for.

You may also want to be at the auction in order to try to up the price a bit yourself. This sort of thing, of course, goes on at auctions but is usually done by professional 'plants'. What happens is that if the bidding is not going very well, but there is clearly one person who is interested in whatever is being bid for, the 'plant' will bid against him in order to push up the price.

I would not recommend this course of action. If you are not careful you could end up buying your own car and even having to pay more for it than your reserve!

Miscellaneous information

Abandoned vehicles

Local authorities are empowered to remove any vehicle which is, or appears to be, abandoned on a public highway. So if your car needs attention and has to be left for any length of time, be careful that it is not thought to be abandoned.

The decision as to whether or not a vehicle is abandoned is very much at the discretion of the inspecting officer. If the vehicle is untaxed, the local authority has the right to remove it. Initially, a DVLC check will be carried out by trying to obtain details of the registered keeper through the registration number. Usually, such a check takes two to three weeks. On receipt of the details from DVLC, the local authority will write to the person named as the registered keeper. They must then wait 28 days in order to give the owner of the vehicle an opportunity to respond.

At the end of the 28 days, the local authority will serve a seven-day notice that the car will be broken up if it is not claimed. In the meantime, they will also have contacted the police in order to ensure that the vehicle has not been reported as stolen.

If the vehicle is left in a position in which it is causing an obstruction or in such a way that it may need to be removed urgently, the local authority is empowered to do so, particularly if the vehicle is untaxed. In these circumstances, they must ensure that the vehicle is removed without causing any damage and that it is stored in exactly the same condition as it was in when it was removed. The procedure of contacting the keeper or the owner of the vehicle will then be followed in the normal way. In the meantime, if any damage occurs to the vehicle, the local authority can be held liable.

211

Generally most councils do not have facilities for storing abandoned vehicles and so they will have a contract with a local scrap dealer. The scrap dealer will make a record of the removal or storage costs (where relevant) and, if the vehicle remains unclaimed, the money for the scrap will be likely to cover the cost of removal and other charges. Such an arrangement works quite well with most local authorities.

Although the law is quite clear in respect of abandoned vehicles, different local authorities may have policies which whilst encompassing the law, often give the consumer additional protection. For example, in many cases the local authority will place a notice on an apparently abandoned vehicle. They are not legally obliged to do so but it has been found to be quite effective – that is, from the local authority's point of view. If a notice is placed on the car stating that it appears to be abandoned and that the local authority will remove it if it is not dealt with within a certain time, then obviously the owner of the vehicle is going to do something about it fairly quickly. They may choose to notify the local authority or simply take the car somewhere else. If the vehicle is abandoned then a notice placed on the car is going to be an advertisement to all and sundry to this effect and the result is likely to be a free for all. Anyone needing the odd wheel, wing, engine, seats and so on are likely to see this as a perfect opportunity for them to obtain these parts without upsetting anybody, thus the extent of the obstruction is likely to be reduced considerably over a relatively short period. Nevertheless, what is left will still have to be disposed of and it is often more difficult to move in that condition because it can not be towed and has to be uplifted.

Normally abandoned vehicles are the responsibility of the borough engineer's department although you should consult with your local authority for further information and they will be able to advise you which is the relevant department.

Cherished number plates

A famous comedian has the registration number 'COM 1C' on his car. Many registration marks can spell out things which are relevant to certain people and it is possible to buy such registration marks and to transfer them from one vehicle to another.

It is, however, quite expensive – £80 and that is just the cost of the transfer. You may have to pay the current owner of the registration mark a considerable amount more than that before he will agree to let you have it. In some circumstances you may need to buy the car. For example, if it is old and no registration document is available or if it is unlicensed and will not pass another MOT test. You may need to have the donor vehicle inspected by the local vehicle licensing office and they may also wish to inspect the receiving vehicle.

The first step is to find the registration mark you want. If you do not know the owner of the vehicle you can find out by writing to DVLC. Once you have located the present owner you should find out whether they are willing to sell the registration mark to you. There is not really a going rate of such transactions. It depends on how badly you want the registration mark, and the present owner will be only too aware of this and may try to cash in on it. If the car bearing the registration mark is old and tatty, you may decide that you could get a better deal by simply offering to buy the car.

If the present owner of the vehicle is happy to sell the registration mark to you then you should obtain an application form for the transfer of registration marks (V317) from the local vehicle licensing office. You will need to complete all the details of the donor vehicle together with the details of the receiving vehicle and you will need the agreement and signature of the present owner of the donor vehicle.

Do be sure that it is the owner of the vehicle you are dealing with. Remember that the name shown on the log book as being the registered keeper may not necessarily be the owner of the vehicle. The vehicle could be subject to a hire purchase agreement or owned by a business or company. Make sure you check all of these things carefully before you proceed and certainly before you part with any money or you may find that you have got yourself what you think is a good deal with someone who has no legal right to sell the mark to you.

Once you have returned the V317, the local vehicle licensing office may wish to inspect either or both vehicles, in which case they will notify you of a time and place for the inspection. If the office agrees to the transfer you will be sent a form V351 which explains when you can change the plates and what to do next. If you need any more information, you can contact the local vehicle licensing office which you will find in your telephone book under 'Transport, Department of'.

It usually takes about six to eight weeks for the new registration documents to arrive and once you have obtained your cherished number you can transfer it again to any other vehicle whenever you like.

Seat belts

Laws affecting the motorist saw a variety of changes in 1983. In particular, it became law on the 31 January of that year for drivers and front-seat passengers to wear seat belts. The penalty for failing to wear a seat belt is a £10 fixed penalty ticket. If the case goes to court you may be liable for a £50 fine. Any passenger over the age of 14 risks prosecution and adults are responsible for children below that age. The only exception is if a doctor has issued an exemption certificate (which will cost around £20) and this will only be issued under certain circumstances, like pregnancy and so on. Seat belt wearing is compulsory now in more than 20 countries and the penalties for failure to comply with the law vary enormously, from £3 in Luxemburg to £150 in Australia: New Zealand £4; Norway £5; Belgium £7; France, Spain and the Netherlands £10; Sweden £20; Denmark £100.

Making the wearing of seat belts compulsory is estimated to have reduced road deaths in France by 63 per cent; Sweden by 50 per cent; Australia by 20 per cent; Belgium by 25 per cent; Japan by 65 per cent; Norway by 13 per cent.

So you can see that wearing a seat belt is not just a legal requirement but it also makes good sense. Researchers worldwide say that a person not wearing a seat belt can be killed in a crash when the car is travelling at not more than 12 mph. The impact of a crash at this speed is enough to force you out of your seat at 7 times your own weight. Travelling at 30 mph, the weight becomes several tons.

In a head-on impact, a car travelling at 30 mph is stopped in about one tenth of a second. During this time the body of the car crushes by up to 20 inches while your body continues to travel at roughly 30 mph for what is known as second impact – into the windscreen or steering column or dashboard.

If you are wearing a seat belt you will get a 12–16 inch 'stopping distance' stretching as it holds you from striking part of the car.

A collision travelling at only 6 mph is sufficient to cause a fractured skull.

Experts estimate that there is only a 1 per cent chance of being seriously injured when wearing a seat belt and you are five times safer inside a crashing car than if you were thrown out of it. Generally, the time when you are most likely to forget to 'belt up' is when you are travelling only a very short distance from home, but statistics show that this is precisely the time when you are most likely to have an accident and apart from the risk to yourself and the risk of being prosecuted, you also run the risk of invalidating your insurance. When you take out insurance, part of the contract is that you will be complying with the law and certainly that you will be taking every reasonable precaution for safety. Failure to wear a seat belt is going to affect your claim. There will be a question on the claim form as to whether seat belts were being worn and if the answer is no the insurance company will certainly not treat your claim sympathetically if at all.

Anyone making a claim for a personal injury is likely to have their settlement severely reduced if seat belts are not worn. There have already been precedents in courts establishing the principle that failure to wear a seat belt can be considered contributory negligence, and as a result awards for personal injury claims have been reduced by up to 25 per cent. Since the wearing of seat belts became law, awards can be reduced by up to 30 per cent if it is decided that failure to wear a seat belt amounts to contributory negligence.

In the same way that someone convicted of drinking and driving is likely to be very heavily penalised by the insurance companies in terms of higher premiums, your insurance is likely to be loaded after a claim for an accident if you were not wearing a seat belt.

Common problems

Advice agencies and trading standards departments deal with thousands and thousands of complaints every year about cars. Some of the most common types of problems are illustrated below.

Case study 1

★Young Mr A, thrilled about having just passed his driving test, went to a local dealer to buy a used car. He had been saving hard and was really looking forward to having a car of his own. He knew nothing about cars and made this clear to the dealer when he inspected those that were available.

Eventually he settled on a fairly elderly Mini as being within his price range and apparently fitting all his needs. He took it for a run and all seemed to be well so he agreed to buy it.

He had not brought all his savings with him and explained to the dealer that he would have to come back the next day with all the money. The dealer, however, pointed out that he could have sold the car to someone else in the meantime and insisted that young Mr A left a deposit on the car to show goodwill. Mr A agreed to this, left £100 deposit and obtained a receipt showing the balance to be paid.

That evening, young Mr A told his father how pleased he was about the new car and his father suggested that he go with him the next day to collect it 'just so I can look it over and make sure everything's alright'.

The next day young Mr A, cash in hand, set off with his father to pick up his car. When they got to the dealer Mr A Snr had a look at the car and discovered that there were a number of things wrong with it. He pointed out to his son that whilst one would expect a few minor faults, the faults with this car were fairly serious and would cost quite a lot of money to put right. He explained that what the dealer was asking for the car was simply too much money considering all of the things that were wrong with it, and because Mr A was concerned about his son going out in a car which could be unroadworthy, he forbade him to buy it.

Mr A Snr, then asked the car dealer whether he was prepared to put all of these things right before selling the car and the dealer, naturally enough, said that he was not. Mr A then said 'in that case we don't want it and we'll have the money back.' The dealer refused.

Was young Mr A entitled to have his £100 back? Well unfortunately he was not. Young Mr A had entered into a legally binding contract with the car dealer and he had made no conditions. When he went back the following day and, in essence, had changed his mind, he was in breach of contract and therefore the dealer is entitled to damages. In fact, the dealer would be within his rights to insist on enforcement of the contract and could take Mr A to court for the full amount of the agreed price.

What young Mr A should have done is to leave a deposit making it clear that it was subject to a satisfactory inspection, and that should that inspection not be satisfactory the contract would be at an end and all of his money would be refundable.

Case study 2

★ Mr B spotted a nice looking Renault on a dealer's forecourt one day and decided that this was just the car for him. The next day he went to the dealer, inspected the car and asked to take it out for a test drive. The dealer said that that would be in order but that as Mr B was not insured he would have to drive.

Off they went around the block, chatting away merrily and all seemed to be well. They got back to the dealer's premises, agreed a price and the dealer explained to Mr B that he gave a three-month warranty on all of the cars that he sold. He gave Mr B a receipt for the money he had paid and wrote on the bottom of it 'three months warranty'. Mr B handed over his money and drove off in his new purchase.

Two days later Mr B noticed that the gearbox seemed to be a little stiff and was 'crunching'. He did not worry about it too much at that stage but within a couple of weeks it became clear that there was something not quite right so he returned to the dealer who said 'don't worry guv, it's only a minor adjustment that you need, leave it with me and I'll sort it out under the three-month warranty'. Mr

B left the car there and a couple of days later went back to collect it. The dealer assured Mr B that it was a minor little problem that had now been resolved.

Mr B took the car away and was quite satisfied until a few weeks later when the same problem occurred again. He returned the car to the dealer who this time said that it probably needed a part and he would arrange to get the part for Mr B but in order not to inconvenience him Mr B could continue driving the car until the part was in stock. Mr B thought this was extremely reasonable and agreed to wait until he had a phone call from the dealer saying that the part was now ready to be fitted.

Two more weeks went by and Mr B still had not heard from the dealer so he telephoned to see whether the part had arrived. The dealer said that these parts were not easy to get 'what with being a foreign car' and that he would call him as soon as it was in stock.

A further month went by and Mr B telephoned again. This time he was told that the part had arrived and that the dealer had just not got around to telephoning him. It was agreed that he would take the car in the following day to be fitted.

Mr B subsequently took the car back to the dealer who said that he would phone Mr B as soon as the car was ready. A week went by with no call from the dealer so Mr B phoned him. The dealer said that he had been a bit busy that week and had not had time to do it but he promised that it would be fixed this week for sure. At the end of the week, Mr B phoned again and this time was told that the car was ready to collect. Mr B picked up the car and was assured that all would now be well.

Within a week it was obvious that there was something very seriously wrong with the gearbox and this time Mr B was getting annoyed. He decided that rather than take the car back to the dealer he would get it checked by somebody else so, as he was a member of the AA, he arranged for them to inspect the car.

The report from the AA clearly indicated that the gearbox was absolutely useless and would have to be replaced. This was going to be a very expensive job so, armed with a copy of the report, Mr B went back to the dealer and demanded that he replace the gearbox once and for all. The dealer, however, pointed out that his three-month warranty had now expired and that if he wanted the gearbox replaced he was going to have to pay for it. Mr B thoroughly dissatisfied with this, argued but to no avail. He then said that if the dealer was not prepared to replace the gearbox free of charge then he wanted to have all his money back and if necessary he would take him to court and he would also be claiming the cost of the AA report. The dealer simply laughed in his face.

Poor Mr B could take the dealer to court and he could try claiming the cost of the AA report as well but I am afraid that he would lose. Unfortunately, Mr B had made a number of very fundamental mistakes.

To begin with, Mr B did not drive the car himself when they went for a test drive and, of course, the dealer was able to jiggle about with that gear stick in order to disguise any faults. The next problem is that when Mr B realised there was something wrong with the gearbox, he accepted the dealer's offer to 'put it right' without question.

Although the dealer had given Mr B a three-month warranty, Mr B did not have to accept repairs under that warranty. The Sale of Goods Act says that Mr B is entitled to reject the car if it is defective and have all of his money back and he should not have been dissuaded from doing so because of a so-called guarantee. The dealer obviously knew there was something seriously wrong with the gearbox and simply kept quiet.

The major problem here is that Mr B did not get the AA to look over the car until it was too late. As he was a member of the AA, then he should have asked them to inspect the car *before* he handed over any money and naturally he would not then have bought it.

His final big mistake was in allowing the dealer to carry out repairs to the vehicle because once he had done that he had lost his right to reject it and ask for his money back and all he could claim was damages.

This is what Mr B should have done. Obviously he should have arranged for the AA to inspect if before he bought it. Even so, as soon as he noticed there was something wrong with the gearbox he should have returned to the dealer and rejected the car, insisting upon his money back. If the dealer offered to repair the car under warranty then Mr B could have agreed to this 'without prejudice' and he should have written a letter to the dealer to that effect and kept a copy of it. Here is an example of the letter that he should have written:

Dear Sir
On such and such a date I bought a Renault (registration number) from you at a cost of £x.

Within two days I noticed that there was something wrong with the gearbox and I returned the car to you and asked for my money back.

You refused to refund my money and advised me that as you had given me a three-month warranty you would repair the car free of charge.

I am not obliged to accept a repair but I am prepared to do so without prejudice to my legal rights.

If the repair proves unsatisfactory or if anything else goes wrong with the car at a later date, I shall enforce my right to reject it and have my money refunded in full.

Yours faithfully

Mr B would have protected himself by making it clear that he had rejected the car right at the beginning.

His other problem is claiming the cost of the AA report. It would not be reasonable for him to claim this money since he did not advise the dealer in advance that it was his intention to have a report carried out on the car and therefore his claim would not be 'foreseeable' and one is only entitled to claim foreseeable damages. Even at that late stage, he should have written to the dealer pointing out that it was his intention to get the car independently inspected and that if the report indicated that there was something seriously wrong with the car that he would be claiming damages (because he had already lost his right to have his money back), including the cost of the report.

Case study 3

★Mr C bought a used car and a month later, whilst he was driving on a motorway, the car began to lose power and make very unpleasant noises. Mr C continued to drive the car, slowly, until the next exit where he left the motorway and made his way to the nearest garage.

The mechanic inspected the car and told him that the engine was absolutely useless and would have to be replaced.

Mr C was a long way from home and he did not really know what to do. Should he leave the car there to be repaired or should he get it towed back home to be repaired there? He decided in the end that the cost of the towing would be too expensive and that it would be more sensible to let this garage repair the car and he would go home on the train.

Mr C therefore told the garage to go ahead with the repairs and to phone him as soon as it was ready so that he could arange to come back and collect it. He also asked how much it was likely to cost and was told that it would be in the region of £500 to £600.

Mr C went home and the following day got in touch with the dealer from whom he had bought the car, told him what had happened and said that he expected the dealer to foot the bill. The dealer simply said that he had absolutely no intention of paying for a new engine since in his opinion the car did not need a new engine and could probably have been repaired a lot more cheaply. He further told Mr C that he should have arranged to have the car brought back to him and he would have done the repairs free of charge. Mr C said that the towing charges would have been enormous and the dealer said that he would have paid for it. The dealer further pointed out that in his view there was nothing seriously wrong with the engine and that when something went wrong on the motorway Mr C should not have continued to drive it. In doing so, he had caused the engine more damage which is probably why it now needed to be replaced.

Mr C went home and contacted the garage where he had left his car to see whether they could stop work and arrange to have his car towed home. When he spoke to the garage they told him that they had already removed his old engine and were about to fit a new one. They further told him that if they were to stop work they would charge him for the labour they had undertaken so far and they would also make a claim against him for the engine which they had obtained and which they would not now be needing. Mr C realised that if he was going to get stuck with a hefty bill anyway he may as well let them go ahead with the repairs.

Mr C was now stuck with a repair bill of £600 which the supplying dealer was refusing to meet.

It was, of course, perfectly possible that the original dealer had no intention of paying for the car to be towed back or indeed of carrying out any repairs free of charge – never mind fitting a new engine. The problem for Mr C, however, was that he never gave the dealer an opportunity. If he now sued the dealer for the cost of the repair, and the dealer defended the case on the grounds that he would have arranged for the car to be towed back and would have paid for all repairs himself, Mr C would be quite likely to lose his case. A further defence would have been that Mr C was himself responsible for the majority of the damage to the engine because he continued driving it once he knew that there was something wrong instead of stopping immediately before the engine was completely wrecked.

What Mr C should have done as soon as the car broke down was to telephone the dealer and explain what had happened. If the dealer had then refused to do anything about it, it would have been perfectly reasonable for Mr C to go ahead with the repairs and then claim the cost from the dealer on the grounds that he had refused to honour his obligations. He should have confirmed the details of their telephone conversation in writing and kept a copy. If it was not possible to contact the dealer as soon as the car had broken down then he could have asked the garage whether they would be prepared to hang on to the car for him for a day or so until he could contact the supplying dealer to find out what he was prepared to do. He may have incurred a small storage charge for this but it would have safeguarded any claim that he wished to make against the supplying dealer, and, in fact, if he could prove that the car was sold with a defective engine then he would even have been able to reject the car and claim back all of his money from the supplying dealer.

Case study 4

★Mr D was very taken with a BMW on offer in a local showroom. It was a bit outside his price range so the dealer arranged finance for him.

Mr D was very pleased with his new purchase and the monthly repayments were quite manageable.

After he had had the car for nearly two years he decided that it was time to sell it and get a new one. Mr D had done only 13,000 miles in the car and since it was of low mileage when he bought it he considered that this would be a very good selling point.

He advertised the car privately and very soon a buyer came along. Mr D's finance agreement was a personal loan and he decided that he would use the cash that he got for the BMW to put towards another car and continue to pay off the balance on the finance agreement.

About three months after he had sold the BMW he received a letter from the man who bought it (Mr E), telling him that Mr E had been in touch with the previous owner in order to verify the mileage. Apparently, the previous owner said that the car had done a much higher mileage than that which was currently shown on the clock and therefore Mr E expected to have either his money back or damages for the fact that the car had been clocked.

Mr D was horrified and being a man of honour he immediately wrote to Mr E asking how much he wanted. Mr E said he would be prepared to accept £800 and Mr D sent him a cheque immediately.

Mr D then returned to the supplying dealer in order to demand reimbursement on the grounds that the dealer must have clocked the car. Alas, the dealer was no more. He had sold his showroom to someone else and the new owner told Mr D that he accepted absolutely no responsibility at all for anything which had gone on before.

Mr D felt very unhappy about the situation but decided there was nothing further he could do.

Actually, there was something that Mr D could do. Even though the dealer had disappeared, Mr D purchased this car through a finance agreement which was arranged by the dealer and therefore had a debtor–creditor–supplier agreement as defined in the Consumer Credit Act; section 75 of that Act says that the supplier of the finance must accept equal liability with the supplier of the goods. Mr D should have written immediately to the finance company explaining what had happened and claiming the £800 damages that he had had to give to Mr E.

Case study 5

★Mr F saw a car advertised in his local newspaper, and as it was just what he was looking for he got in touch with the seller and arranged to go and examine it.

The car and the price seemed entirely suitable and in some ways it all seemed too good to be true so he asked the seller a number of questions like 'has it ever been involved in an accident?'; 'has it ever undergone any major repairs?' and so on. In all cases the seller replied that he did not know. He explained that he bought the car for his son only a few months earlier because he was learning to drive. He went on to explain that his son failed his driving test and did not think he was up to taking another one. As he had a car of his own he decided to sell this one. Mr F accepted what the seller said and bought the car.

A few days later Mr F took his new purchase into his local garage because the brakes seemed to need some adjustment. The garage said that they would get the car up on the ramp and check the brakes over for him. When they did so, they discovered not only that the brakes were seriously defective but also that there was considerable corrosion underneath the car and that as such it would never get through an MOT test without extensive repairs.

Mr F immediately contacted the seller and said that he wanted his money back.

The seller quite rightly said that he had never made any representations to Mr F about the car, that he had no idea what sort of condition it was in because they had hardly ever used it, and that on that basis he was not prepared to take the car back and give him back his money.

Mr F, concluding that there was nothing further to be done, arranged for his garage to carry out all the repairs which cost him a great deal of money.

Mr F should not have been put off so lightly. Whilst it was true that the seller did not misrepresent the vehicle and therefore any claim along those lines would have been a waste of time, the vehicle was in a dangerous and unroadworthy condition and it was a criminal offence under the Road Traffic Act to sell a car in such a condition. Mr F should have contacted either his local Trading Standards Department or the police who could have arranged to inspect the car and, having found that it was unroadworthy, would have prosecuted the seller.

Having the seller prosecuted would still not have got Mr F his money back, however, although it may have given him a degree of satisfaction. But he could have sued the seller in the county court for breach of contract on the grounds that the car was dangerous and unroadworthy and therefore not fit for the purpose of driving along the road.

Case study 6

★Mr G, needing a new car, decided that it might be quite fun to buy one at an auction as he understood that good deals were to be had this way.

When he got to the auction he found that the cars were packed pretty tightly and that it was very difficult to inspect them to any reasonable degree before the sale. However, he spotted a Volkswagen which he thought would be OK. He felt that a reasonable price would be about £1,000 and decided that he was prepared to bid up to that amount. In fact he was able to get his VW for considerably less than that and was absolutely delighted that he secured it for £600.

He paid his money and was told that he would have to wait until the end of the auction so that they could move out the other cars in order to get to his.

He waited and waited and eventually saw two men pushing his new purchase away from the lot. He went over to them and asked for the keys. He then got in the car and attempted to start it up but to no avail. He immediately went back to the auctioneer and said that the car did not start and that as there was obviously something seriously wrong he wanted his money back. The auctioneer simply laughed at him and said 'this one isn't a runner. It was sold as seen mainly for parts. Nobody said that it would go.' Mr G then asked what he was supposed to do and the auctioneer told him that he did not care but he must arrange for it to be moved otherwise they would charge him storage.

Mr G went to the police who said that it was nothing to do with them as this was a civil claim.

What the auctioneer did was perfectly legal.

Mr G should have carefully examined the terms and conditions of the auction and he should have asked a few relevant questions about this car before he began bidding for it. It is quite common for cars to be sold 'as seen' at auction and there is absolutely no guarantee that they will go. It is quite possible that the car may not even have had an engine in it. Mr G had just made a very big and expensive mistake.

Case study 7

★Mr and Mrs A purchased a car from a dealer who arranged credit for them. The credit agreement was hire purchase. The car was a new car and Mr A arranged for the insurance cover over the telephone, via his broker. The broker arranged to send him a cover note immediately so that he was able to drive the car and at the same time sent him a proposal form for completion and return to the insurance company.

In the meantime, Mrs A went to her local vehicle licensing office to arrange to have the log book transferred. As she did this in person, she completed the form and signed it.

When the insurance proposal form arrived, with the cover note, Mr A completed it ensuring that all of the information was correct and returned it to the insurance company with a cheque for the appropriate amount of the premium.

All was well for nearly two years and then they were involved in an accident which was not their fault.

The other driver, however, was drunk and driving a stolen vehicle thus he had no insurance cover. Mr and Mrs A, though sorry that they would lose their no claims bonus, nevertheless considered themselves fortunate that they had fully comprehensive insurance (as they were obliged to do whilst they had a hire purchase agreement).

When Mr A completed the claim form he answered all the questions correctly, he thought, but one of the questions asked the name of the registered keeper of the vehicle and he put his own name. Another question asked who was the owner of the vehicle (if different from above) and he put 'as above'.

Some time later he was advised by the insurance company that they were not honouring his claim – despite the fact that he had fully comprehensive insurance and that he was entirely blameless in respect of the accident, because of 'nondisclosure of a material fact'. On receipt of this letter he immediately telephoned the insurance company and asked them what this alleged non-disclosure was. He was advised that he was not the registered keeper but that his wife was named as the registered keeper (because the vehicle had been a total loss the insurance company had asked to be sent the log book – this is normal practice).

Naturally, Mr A protested bitterly and pointed out that whilst most of the documentation was in his name, this was a 'family car'; that as far as he was concerned the car belonged to both of them. He further pointed out that the only reason the log book was in her name and the other documents in his name was because Mrs A had arranged for the car to be re-registered simply to save him taking time off work (vehicle licensing offices are not open at particularly convenient times).

The insurance company then agreed on the basis of this information to reconsider their decision.

Several more weeks went by and he received a further letter advising him that whilst they were satisfied with his explanation and would in fact have been prepared to accept it, they were still not going to meet his claim on the grounds of a further non-disclosure.

Again Mr A telephoned the insurance company to find out what they now considered he had done wrong. The insurance company then pointed out that with regard to the question 'who is the legal owner of the vehicle if different from above?' Mr A had said that he was the owner of the vehicle when in fact it belonged to a finance company as it was the subject of a hire purchase agreement.

Mr A's claim was not met and he lost several thousand pounds. He also had to pay the balance outstanding on the finance agreement even though he had no car.

Mr and Mrs A had not acted in any way dishonestly. The mistakes which they made were only as a result of their failure to understand fully the implications of the finance agreement or of the insurance company's interpretation of material facts.

Case study 8

★Mr A decided to sell his car. It was in excellent condition and he had always taken good care of it. He advertised it in the local paper and waited for a response.

He had a number of replies to his advertisement but, as is often the case in this situation, only three people actually turned up to look at the car. One of them decided that it was not quite what he had in mind. The second person wanted a little more time to think about it whilst the third person (Mr B) was suitably impressed and wanted to do business. Mr B asked Mr A if he had all of the relevant documents relating to the car. Mr A assured him that he had and said that he would fetch them. At the same time Mr B said that he would just wander out and have another look at the bodywork.

Mr A came out of the house carrying all of the relevant documents and Mr B was looking around the car. Mr B then asked whether they could get into the car to see whether it was comfortable. Mr A agreed and unlocked the car and they both got inside, Mr B in the driver's seat and Mr A in the passenger seat. Mr B inspected the documents – the log book, MOT certificate and even the service history together with a variety of receipts.

Mr A and Mr B were getting on famously at this stage and Mr B appeared more than satisfied with all of the documents that he was shown. He placed them on the dashboard and then asked Mr A whether he could take the car for a test drive. Mr A said that would be perfectly in order and handed Mr B the keys. Remember that at this stage they are both sitting in Mr A's car, Mr B in the driver's seat.

Mr B then put the key in the ignition and started up the engine. Just as he was about to pull away he suddenly switched off the car and said 'oh dear, I've just thought, I don't want to leave my own car unattended at the roadside because the driver's door doesn't lock properly and I have left things inside it'. Mr B then asked whether Mr A would be prepared to wait with his car while he took Mr A's car for a 'quick run around the block'. Mr A had found Mr B a very pleasant fellow and saw no reason not to oblige, given that Mr A after all had Mr B's car. Thus Mr A vacated his own car with the keys to Mr B's car and off drove Mr B.

After waiting more than an hour Mr A was becoming alarmed to say the least and after nearly three hours he finally decided to phone the police in case Mr B had been involved in an accident whilst driving Mr A's car. The policeman was neither surprised nor sympathetic. He told Mr A that he had heard a story like this before and asked Mr A for the registration number of Mr B's car which, he felt sure, would be listed as a stolen vehicle. Mr A then went and checked the registration number, gave it to the policeman and waited while the policeman checked it. Sure enough, the car which Mr A now had in his possession was a stolen vehicle and the policeman advised him that he should hang on to the keys whilst the rightful owner was notified of its whereabouts. It had, in fact, only been reported stolen that very morning. Mr A was further advised by the policeman that they would now record his car as a stolen vehicle.

In the meantime, Mr B had taken Mr A's car straight to a car dealer. This was in fact Mr B's second visit to the car dealer because he had been there earlier that day expressing a desire to sell his car and asking whether the dealer would be interested in it. (All of the information that he needed about the car had of course appeared in Mr A's advertisement.) The dealer had said that he would be prepared to buy the car following inspection and if they could agree a price. Mr B had said that he would be prepared to accept less than the book price as he was in a hurry to sell.

When Mr B arrived at the garage with the car, the dealer immediately carried out an HPI check (this is a check which a dealer can do instantly through a company called HP Information in order to ensure that the vehicle is not the subject of a hire purchase agreement). Of course the check proved satisfactory and Mr B presented all of the documents giving his name and address as that of Mr A (the name shown on the log book, the MOT certificate and all of the service documents). The dealer was quite satisfied with the condition of the vehicle and that all of the documents were in order and furthermore he considered he had got a pretty good price as Mr B had already said that he needed to sell the car quickly.

Mr B left the garage with cash in his hand and in his wake left two stolen vehicles. The dealer would have been unable to pass title of the vehicle to anyone else that he sold it to. However, although the vehicle had been reported as stolen, it could remain on his forecourt for some time and indeed another consumer come along and buy the car. It could be some time later before the purchaser was stopped by the police as being in possession of a stolen vehicle. That purchaser would have a claim against the garage for a refund of the purchase price on the grounds of breach of contract (there is an implied condition in every contract that the seller has title to the goods). The dealer would then have been out of pocket (always assuming that he chose to honour his legal obligations and pay back the innocent purchaser – he may have chosen instead, of course, to go into liquidation or just disappear).

Now let us go back to Mr A – he reported this stolen vehicle to his insurance company and they made him an offer. It was considerably less than the price that he and Mr B had agreed, but nevertheless he felt he had no choice but to accept it. The rightful owner of the other car had now turned up and reclaimed it and so Mr A considered himself also out of pocket. But now, of course, the police had recovered Mr A's vehicle and notified him to this effect. Mr A pointed out that his insurance company had paid his claim but that he would really rather have his car back.

Can the police release it to him? The answer is no. Once the insurance company had met Mr A's claim, the car became their property. However, the innocent purchaser, who did not manage to get his money back from the car dealer who in fact chose to go into liquidation, was now arguing that the car was his property and throughout all of this, the car remained impounded by the police. It was now for either the insurance company or the innocent purchaser (or indeed Mr A or the car dealer) to take the police to court for a magistrate to decide on who had title to the vehicle.

It is likely that the magistrate would have decided that title went to the insurance company and that every other party may have had various damages claims; whether or not they would have been able to secure such claims was not the problem of the magistrate.

Case study 9

★ Mr A bought a used car from a car dealer. The vehicle had an MOT certificate but was not taxed and the car dealer told him that the registration document (log book) had been sent away to DVLC and had not come back yet. Mr A was advised by the car dealer to return in a few days when the log book would no doubt be there.

Mr A returned as advised and the log book still had not arrived. Mr A was worried that he was not going to be able to tax the car without the log book. So he kept pestering the dealer. Eventually, the dealer got so fed up with this that he told him he would put it in the post to him as soon as it arrived and to stop bothering him.

The log book never arrived and shortly after that Mr A was stopped by the police and asked to produce his documents at a police station. He was advised when stopped that because the vehicle was not displaying a tax disc he would be prosecuted for that.

When Mr A went to the police station with his insurance certificate and the MOT certificate he explained that he did not have a log book and that the reason that the car was not taxed was because the car dealer did not supply the log book. Poor Mr A was prosecuted for not having any tax.

The fact is that Mr A did not have a leg to stand on and pleading ignorance was no excuse. First of all it is possible to tax a vehicle without a log book. You simply apply to a local vehicle licensing office. Secondly, Mr A could easily have applied for a new log book.

All he had to do was to pop along to his local post office and pick up form V62 which is an application for a registration document. Having completed the application form he could have sent it off to the DVLC and waited for a new registration document to be sent direct to him.

Useful addresses

Association of Credit Unions Limited
PO Box 35, Credit Union Centre, High Street, Skelmersdale
Lancashire WN8 8AP 0695-31444

The Automobile Association (AA)
Fanum House, The Broadway, Stanmore,
Middlesex 01-954 7373

Department of Transport
2 Marsham Street, London SW1T 3EB 01-212 3434

Driver and Vehicle Licensing Centre (DVLC)
Swansea SA99 1AL★
Driver: 0792-72151
Vehicle: 0792-72134
(★Post Code varies according to the nature of the enquiry.)

Institute of Advanced Motorists
IAM House, 359 Chiswick High Road,
London W4 4HS 01-994 4403

Insurance Brokers Registration Council
15 St Helens Place, London EC3 01-588 4387

Motor Agents Association Ltd (MAA)
73 Park Street, Bristol BS1 5PS 0272-293232

Motor Schools Association of Great Britain
167 Langworthy Road, Salford M6 5PW 061-736-1515

National Federation of Credit Unions
5th Floor, Provincial House, Bradford BD1 1NP
0274-753507

The Royal Automobile Club (RAC)
RAC House, Lansdowne Road, Croydon,
Surrey CR9 2JA 01-686 3691

Scottish Motor Trade Association Ltd (SMTA)
3 Palmerston Place, Edinburgh EH12 5AQ 031-225 3643

Society of Motor Manufacturers & Traders Ltd (SMMT)
Forbes House, Halkin Street, London SW1X 7DS
01-235 7000

Vehicle Builders and Repairers Association (VBRA)
Belmont House, 102 Finkle Lane, Gildersome, Leeds LS27
7TW Morley 0532-53833

Vehicle Inspection Division
Department of Transport, Private Car Testing Branch,
Tollgate House, Houlton Street, Bristol BS2 9DJ
0272-662855

Index